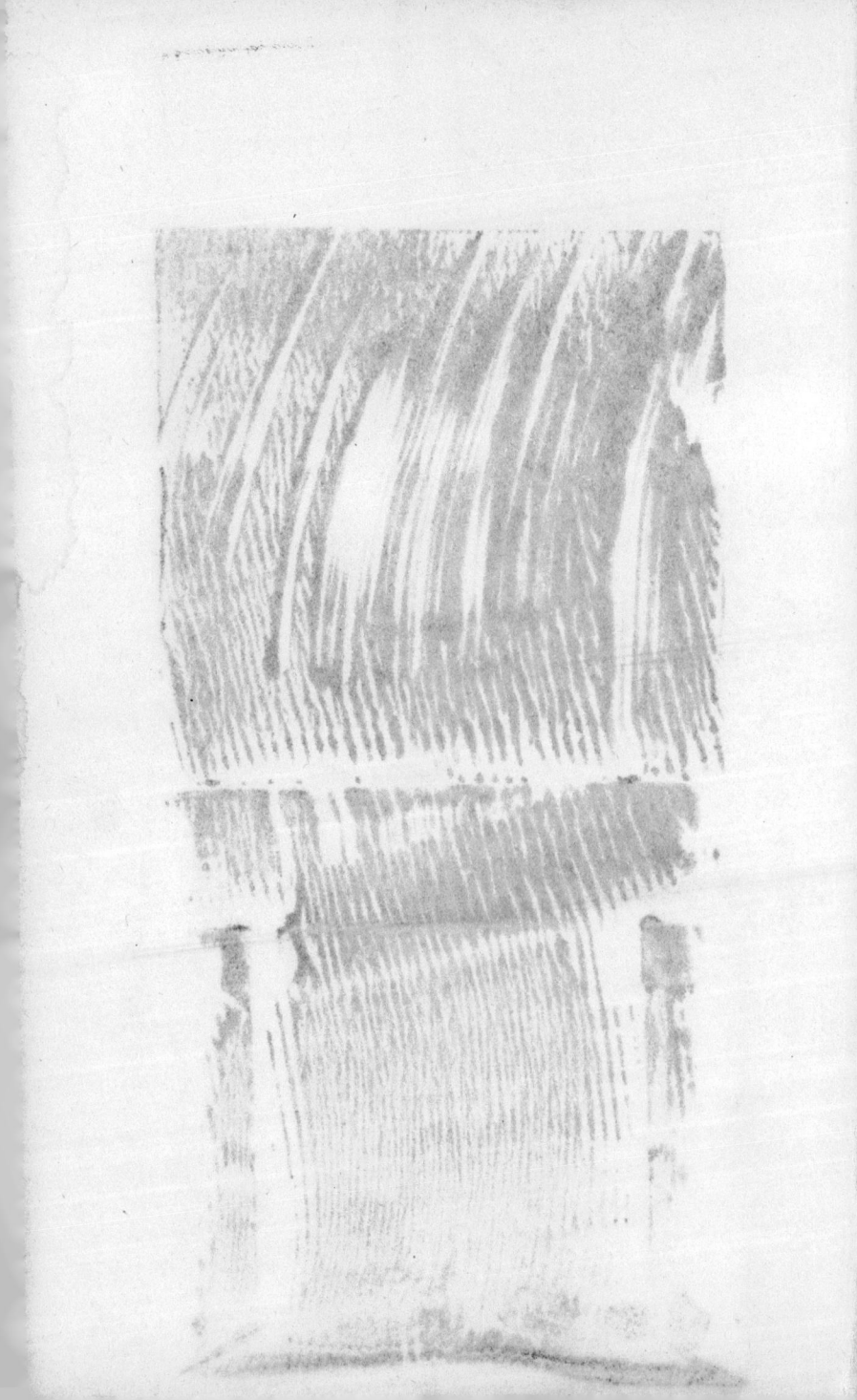

THE BEGINNER'S GUIDE TO SAILING

List of books by the same author:
Beginner's Guide to Swimming and Water Sports
The Young Person's Nature Guide
Concise Herbal Encyclopedia
Herb-growing for Health
Herbal Teas for Health and Pleasure
How to Defeat Rheumatism and Arthritis
How to Keep your Hair on
Herbs for Cooking and Healing
Textbook of Botanic Medicine (viii vols)
Degree Course in Philosophy
Astrology, Palmistry and Dreams
Handbuch der Heilkräuter
Luonnonvaraista Terveysteetä
A Complete Guide to Alternative Healing

THE BEGINNER'S GUIDE TO SAILING

by

DONALD LAW

*Ph.D., D.B.M., Dip.D., Psy.D.,
D.Litt., M.N.T.A., phil. med.D.*

Illustrated by Patty Johns

DRAKE PUBLISHER INC.
NEW YORK
1975

ISBN 0-87749-739-7

Published in 1975 by
DRAKE PUBLISHERS INC.
381 Park Avenue South
New York, N.Y. 10016

© Donald Law

Printed in Great Britain

List of Contents

1	The aims of this book	7
2	The Call of the Waters	10
3	So you Want a Boat: how to buy a boat, what to look out for	15
4	Moorings, Anchors and the like: how to leave them; how to come back; rowing a boat at sea; how to get to your boat at mooring offshore; how to hoist sail; launching from a leeward shore	49
5	Dinghies and Racing	61
6	Three Points of Sailing: running; reaching, close hauled	66
7	Theory of Sailing: the ways of the wind; the Beaufort Scale; a tide in the affairs of men; clues in the clouds; time and tide wait for no man	82
8	Navigation: electronic aids; storms; what to do	96
9	Safety Check List	122
10	Collision: Rule of the Road at Sea	124
11	Inboard Engine Check List	126
	Outboard Motors Check List	127
12	Maintenance and Repairs: hitches, knots and bends	130
13	Clothing: what to wear; stores; what to take with you	141
14	Health, Hygiene and Diet: insurance; vital information	147
15	On joining a club	152
16	Bibliography: other books you might like to read	154
17	Glossary of Nautical Terms	155

Dedication

Werner und Elfriede Taufenbach
Ulf und Karin Stickdorn

Hilpt mi, Sünn un Wind,
Hilpt mi bit Fischen!
Ik heet Klaus Mees
Un bün van Finkwarder.
Finkwarder blifft Finkwarder
Un geiht ne van de See
(Gorch Fock).

John and Pat Shillingford
Edward Storer
Janneke Hindriksen

. . . . My purpose holds
To sail beyond the sunset, and the baths
Of all the western stars until I die.
(Tennyson).

The Aims of This Book

I want to give beginners a good idea of sailing; what boats are, how they function, and how they are managed.

Some works are so full of scientific and technical details that one feels one would have to be a nuclear scientist to go aboard, moreover cast off. I do not like *blinding* readers *with science*, and have omitted as much technical jargon as possible. For anybody who is interested enough to proceed to the mathematical side of sailing it will still be there—at a later stage.

I knew a man who sailed a boat, using his feet only, having lost both his arms in a war. I have known an extremely good sailor who, literally with a book in hand, set forth in a second-hand boat on a lake 100 km. across, 80 km. wide, and taught himself how to sail.

There are many experts, ocean-going yachtsmen and others, who may feel inclined to belittle a simplified approach, but the object of this work is to bring people to a real enjoyment of sailing boats. I cannot foresee how far any reader will take it. Maybe he will emulate some clipper race like that of the *Thermopylae* and *Cutty Sark*, perhaps go solitary fishing like Crabbe's *Peter Grimes*, or exploring like Columbus, and some day writing, as he did: *11th October. At 2 hours after midnight the land was sighted at a distance of 2 leagues.*

There is, and always will be, a great poetry and sense of freedom about the sea, but the first step to explore this is usually learning how to handle a small dinghy on a lake, a sleepy river, or up and down some creek; learn slowly but learn well; courage is the effort by a person who knows what he is doing, foolhardiness takes a risk without understanding what the risk really is.

I have dealt fleetingly with navigation, because this is something *better learnt on the water in the company of an expert* than from a book. To study it from a book without the examples in front of you is like trying to teach a blind man to paint in oils. I have contented myself by explaining the general theory of the subject. However good you get, remember nobody knows it all and even an Admiral can get promoted, as Morley Roberts' story showed!

Sailing is a joy which is timeless: *Unmooring his craft, he spreads the sails to the winds, at the motion of which even the stars which are said to be fixed in the skies above seem to shake.* That was written by Lucan, nearly 2,000 years ago, but the excitement is still felt by every beginner who starts out on his own first solo voyage.

Hints on buying a boat, what to equip her with, how to handle her, insurance, clothing to wear, maintenance, how to survive storms, how to read clouds, winds, and forecast weather, the care of inboard and outboard engines, safety precautions, and a detailed glossary of nautical terms are included, the keynote being ready reference in an easy-to-read style.

THE
BEGINNER'S GUIDE
TO
SAILING

A*

The Call of the Waters

When we were boys we promised that we would venture with our lives, out upon the ocean, and so we performed our promise. This was written over 1000 years ago; it comes from *Beowulf*, the oldest poem in the English language: Its message holds good for generations after, for girls now as well as boys.

The waters of the world cover over 70% of the surface of this planet, some being fresh, others salt. Learning to sail is using them to unite continents rather than divide. There are gentle rivers where we may follow Ratty's commendation in Kenneth Grahame's *Wind in the Willows,* just *messing about in boats,* enjoying the heron's flight across the mirror of the mudflats aglow with morning sunrise. There are seas that team with mystery and excitement. Sailing can take us to Lisbon, of which the Portuguese poet says, the city lies *with seaweed in her hair, and gulls upon her shoulders*: by sea, too, perhaps to the perfumed beauty of the Far East, as the old tar asks (in Boyd Cable's *Tramps*) have you *ever seen a pink sea of cherry blossom with old Fujiyama rising out of it, with the snow spread on the top of the cone and down the sides of the peak, like sugar icing on a Christmas cake?*

In some book we may read that the average cubic mile of seawater contains 128 million tons of salt, some 25 tons of gold, 45 tons of silver, 7 tons of uranium and 500,000 tons of lime! But it is more than that; there is a quality of eternity, a suspicion of magic and ever-present excitement there. It turns boys into men, and men into mariners.

Many authorities alarm and confuse beginners with horror stories about the difficulties of navigation, yet Airas Tinoco, a young page of Prince Henry, the navigator, after 22 members of the crew had been murdered by natives of Guinea with poisoned arrows, brought back a large, (and by today's standards) unwieldly ship safely to Portugal with five totally inexperienced young men. He had barely a scraping knowledge of navigation, learning as he tried! (The writings of Gomez Eannes de Zurara 1410-74). There is much to learn, but little that is impossible, and much that is easier to acquire through practice rather than through textbook exercises.

Whether it is the works of Arthur Ransom, Joseph Conrad or Taffrail that inspire us, always there is the beckoning hand of imagination calling us to the wonder of gliding across the waters in the glare of the midday sun, when, in Swinburne's words, we can perceive *the wind's feet shining along the sea*. In *The Lonely Sea and the Sky* Sir Francis Chichester, writing of an early voyage under sail, remarks. *The magic of the voyage was in my blood. It was sheer joy to set or trim a sail—it was sport getting over the difficulties.*

Yes, there are some difficulties, and there are dangers, for those who do not learn to sail or navigate properly, but in the words of William Hazlitt (1778-1830): *Danger is a good teacher, and makes an apt scholar*. This does not mean that we all have to be as tough as John Masefield's Bill Harker whose hardness shamed the devil himself (*A Tarpaulin Muster*), but it does mean that a sailor must be intelligent and coolheaded. Toughness comes from a great deal of firsthand experience, but with a little effort everybody can behave intelligently and school themselves to be disciplined.

There is something else that sailing does for us, regardless of our age: it gives us an unrivalled sense of freedom; many people find themselves bound in by the demands of society and the economics of earning a living; they seem to echo Milton's *Samson Agonistes* when he cries:

> *In power of others, never in my own,*
> *Scarce half I seem to live, dead more than half.*

But freedom is never mere privilege; it is a sense of responsibility to yourself and to others. It is not wise to sail in the spirit of the naughty young joker in W. W. Jacobs' story *Smoked Skipper*, of whom the captain sadly reported: *He's got a fancy for being a pirate, so just to oblige his father, I told him we was a pirate. He wouldn't have come if I hadn't.*

I will not pretend to tell you *all* there is to know about sailing and the waters upon which we sail. I doubt whether any one man knows, or ever could know, all, but I can explain much, and I can give you the feel of the thing. Boys and men who would scarce dare raise their voices ashore will sometimes sing for joy to themselves or to their mates when afloat, as Oppian, the Greek writer, reported as long ago as A.D. 180: *The fishers raising the loud song of victory, sped the boat with their oars, making the sea echo with their raucous shanty and the rhythmic slap of their blades.* (In those days it was oars, not auxiliary outboards.)

Sailing can help you share the comradeship of fine men, link you with traditions that transcend time and generation gaps. Sesostris in the 16th century B.C. is credited with the invention of the first long boat on the river Nile. The ancient sails resembled the length of towel or sheet which many a boy may hoist to get his home-made raft across a local pond, but it worked. And naval warfare was first recorded several centuries B.C. Mankind learns, but does not always use his knowledge for positive, constructive things. One can sail to adventure, one can sail for relaxation and pleasure, and one can use a sailboat for racing; all sorts of distances, all sorts of conditions, it is an activity which never palls, because the waters, whether fresh or salt, are always changing. This book explains a lot of these changes, and how they affect you, your boat, and how you can use the changes for your own advantage or increased safety.

Sailing has four component parts—the waves, the wind, the boat and you. The first three will behave fairly consistently; (indeed one manual on how to sail in stormy weather went so far as to say there would be less trouble if the yachtsman would go down to his bunk, leaving the boat and her warps to weather the storm, this being likely to minimise the chance of capsize!). This book also seeks to help you understand yourself so that you will not panic in any emergency on the water.

Many of the difficulties afloat are caused by the mariner, or as Herman Melville put it: *Moby Dick seeks thee not. It is thou, thou that madly seekest him.* Just as every motorist is not cut out to be a Grand Prix driver, not every yachtsman will be a Kenichi Horie, Chay Blyth, Knox Johnson or Sir Francis Chichester.

However poetic we may wax about the water, it is never

poetic about us; we either succeed by using the rules of man's accumulated knowledge of sailing (95%), plus a little bit of God's Grace or luck (call it what you will, but don't rely upon that exceeding a narrow 5%) or we fail—it is as simple as all that.

Zeal is no substitute for efficiency. Doing things properly is quite enough, don't be like Masefield's ambitious Jimmy Hicks, who caused his ship to sink (with all hands) by stopping to take a third half hitch when only two were needed!

This book explains how the winds and the waves react; how the slot of the sail produces motions in different directions; how the keel or centreboard can modify the direction of the boat's course. The nature of sails, their treatment and repair are explained. How to buy a boat when you get that *Westward Ho* feeling that Kingsley's Amyas Leigh followed in search of fame and fortune (many a sailor achieves fame, but I'm not so sure of the fortune). The significance of the different rigs is set out with notes and illustrations that enable you to see at a glance which is most suitable for the type of sailing you want.

In reading some accounts of great feats of sailing it is easy to be over-awed by the expensive equipment some of the great yachtsmen took with them, but remember the intrepid 23-year-old Japanese Kenichi Horie who sailed 5,000 miles across the almost unknown North Pacific route from Osaka to San Francisco in a 19 ft. *Mermaid*, built of Plywood averaging one-third of an inch thick. He wrote in his book *Kodoku*: *A young man should not be content to live a life in which his future and security are all assured by the escalator process. I knew I wanted to go to sea, and I didn't need a college education for that.* He navigated with so few instruments and gadgets (he couldn't afford any more) that his surviving five storms (including a typhoon) was miraculous.

They keynote of this work is that no instruments or gadgets can ever be a substitute for good seamanship. It is better to be able to take a really accurate sextant reading than to rely solely on a lot of expensive equipment than can break down five miles off coast during a mist and leave you helpless.

Sailing helps to clear one's mind, and to distinguish

between dreams and the realities of life, between the club sailors, who spend much of their time in the clubroom, enjoying conviviality, fitting their craft out, and sailing one or two weeks a year, and the men who really do things (they usually wear rugged woolly hats instead of peaked caps).

Robin Lee Graham set out to sail round the world when he was 16 (but by then an experienced lad, very good at navigation). He took five years to do it, and in his book *Dove*, tells of his great adventures and of the beauty he saw. Once you can sail well the world is your oyster, which you can open for yourself.

Perhaps sailing offers us not merely a chance to learn about the art, about the wind and the waves, or about the wide world, but still more about ourselves and the eternal values of life. Perhaps this is the intangible lure that words can only hint at rather than truly express.

The effortless glide into harbour during an orange sunset when the waters burns with reflected red sunfire; the cold misty departure in the early morning to catch the tide; the flap of sailcloth, the slap of sheets in the wind; the lazy, hot, becalmed stretches when one gazes at the water because there is nothing else to do. . . . These are moments you will never forget.

Go sailing, young man (or girl!) you will never regret it, for it is the most wonderful sport of them all!

Donald Law
Ph.D., D.B.M., Dip.D., Psy.D.,
D.Litt., M.N.T.A., phil. med.D.

So you Want a Boat?

You have heard the siren song that Masefield names *the call of the running tide, a wild call and a clear call that may not be denied.*

All that remains is to decide what you are going to sea in, and how you will get it. Begging a boat is made difficult by the amount of competition; there are more applicants than boats to go round: Borrowing a boat is often a short cut to losing one's friends: Stealing boats may cause you to end up with a length of chain tightly wound around your windpipe, many fathoms deep (unless the law rescues you from the boat owner and takes you to a comparatively safe prison for a stretch): Apart from lucky Klaus Tommerup in *Voyage of the Wild Duck* by Holger Drachmann (1846-1908) I have never heard of anybody getting a yacht as a gift: All that remains is to buy one ... but how to buy? and what?

An hour or two beside the river or on the seashore will soon show you that there are many different types of sailing boat, and it is clearly the way you spend your money that determines how much you will have left to enjoy the boat with when you finally make your choice.

Boats are primarily purposeful things, and with the exception of some plastic and chromium *gin palaces* found at some boat shows (the shame of it) most craft are designed for one purpose above others.

A boat intended for a day's fishing expedition offshore differs as much from an ocean-going racer as the latter differs from a week-end cruiser.

The second-hand market is as tricky as that for cars. With a second-hand car you can stop, get out and open the bonnet to try to put things right. But with subaqua-gear this is not practical in a force 9 gale, because if the boat doesn't go straight down she will not stay put long enough to let you seek out a repair manual and figure out what is wrong. The more you learn about boats *before* you buy the less disappointment you will experience. Do not assume that a large sum of money necessarily buys you a better boat, nor that a boat

SLOOP

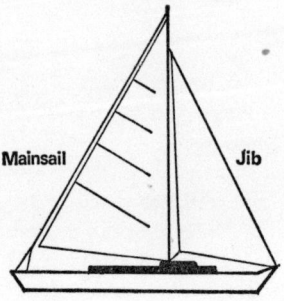

BERMUDA RIG

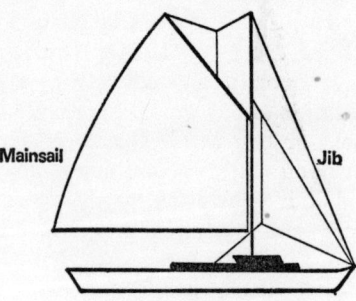

GAFF RIG

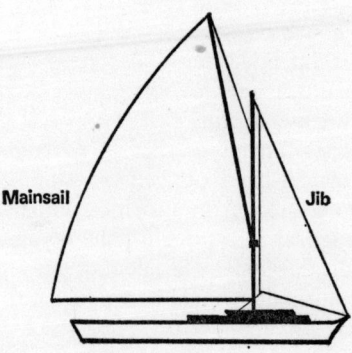

GUNTER RIG

built to your specifications (this for budding naval architects) will end up resembling your specifications. Sir Francis Chichester had some caustic remarks about the inherent vices of Gypsy Moth IV, although she was in a price range to which few of us can aspire!

The types of sail are legion, but here are illustrated descriptions of some of the most common rigs with notes on their suitability for certain conditions. If the language gets a bit too nautical for you refer to the glossary on page 155.

The *Rig* means the way in which mast, sails and their cordage (ropes) are arranged.

A word of warning—an ancient mariner once told me that there is no such thing as a perfect boat, but that boats are like a wife; you look for your ideal and then settle down to live with the compromise most like your ideal.

THE SLOOP

1. An easy boat to handle up to 6 tons; above that it can be awkward especially when heaving to.
2. More accommodation below because of the position of the mast.
3. It is fore and aft rigged on a single mast. It has only one sail fore, but a cutter has two sails fore.
4. A sloop usually carries a mainsail and a jib.
5. It can take a staysail.
6. The mast is further fore than in a cutter.
7. The beam is broader in ratio to keel than in a cutter.
8. Often found with a centreboard and a fixed bowsprit.
9. In the U.S.A. there is seldom any fine distinction between sloop and cutter.
10. Generally speaking a sloop plunges too easily when going headlong into a steep, rough sea (you might sail for years without meeting the condition). To avoid this some designers have brought the mast further backwards (aft) into the boat (this is the true position of the mast in a cutter) and the ungainly word *sl/utter* has been used by some experts to describe it.

THE CUTTER

1. Has a single mainsail, but two sails fore, the jib and the

18 THE BEGINNER'S GUIDE TO SAILING

CUTTER

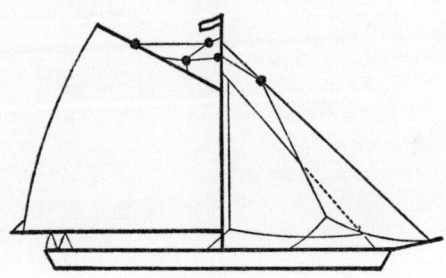

GAFF RIG

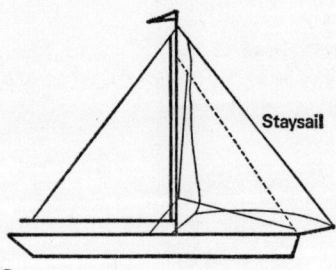

TYPICAL CUTTER RIG

Mast at more of a sloop position

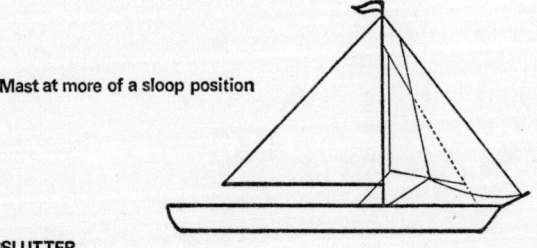

SLUTTER

forestaysail at the bowsprit.
2. The mast is further back than in a sloop (usually just over $\frac{1}{3}$ back from its bowsprit).
3. It has a slender beam in ratio to its draught.
4. Because of the comparative speed of the boat it was a design much favoured in olden times by revenue men chasing smugglers, etc.
5. Nowadays the typical rig approaches the Bermudan, but it may tend to have a lower mast. It is not now considered a fast boat, but more a casual craft.
6. Modern cutter designs occasionally lack the true bowsprit.
7. It is more seaworthy in heavy seas than a sloop.
8. Because of the balance given by triangular sails fore and aft the cutter is held to be very efficient to windward.
9. The rig can become very difficult to handle in large cutters if the boom is very long.

THE KETCH
1. Possibly developed from the old Turkish *qaiq*, thence through the Dutch *Kits*, and French *Carche* to the popular yacht of today.
2. Two-masted vessel. Mainmast and mizzenmast, but this mizzen is larger than that found on a yawl (q.v.).
3. The mizzen is forward of the steering and carries a larger sail than the mizzen of a yawl.
4. Very good in a stiff breeze but not wholly efficient if sailing windward.
5. Not a very fast rig, but much more efficient if full-length battens are used in the sail.
6. The advantage of a ketch is that it allows the use of jib and mizzen without using the mainsail; particularly when entering or leaving harbour, etc.
7. This is called the *old man's rig* because it is easily handled by one man, especially by older sailors, many of whom retire from the Navy to make their home on a boat, and still sail around a bit.

It is very popular for cruising, the area of each sail being smaller, so that it is more easily handled in difficult weather conditions.

THE BEGINNER'S GUIDE TO SAILING

KETCH

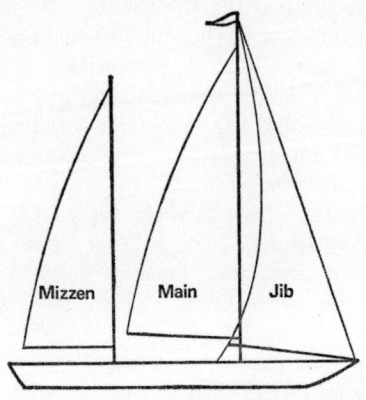

BERMUDAN RIG

BERMUDAN RIG WITH TWO SAILS FORE

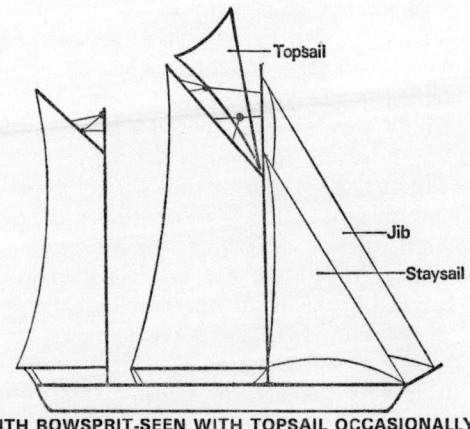

GAFF RIG WITH BOWSPRIT-SEEN WITH TOPSAIL OCCASIONALLY

THE YAWL

1. This is also a two-masted vessel with a *small* mizzen mast abaft the rudder head. The position further aft and shorter mizzen mast distinguish this from the ketch.
2. It is popular for cruising and for some ocean racing!
3. It is nevertheless slower than a cutter in the opinion of most sailors.
4. The yawl has a good performance to windward due to the small mizzen which holds its head windward.
5. Using a sea anchor it is a fairly good craft for riding out a gale.
6. The rig sails closer to the wind than a ketch usually can.
7. The main boom was usually shorter in the original Dutch *jol*, from which it is derived.

THE SCHOONER

1. The mainmast is aft (so a schooner is like a ketch back to front).
2. Very fast if the wind is abaft or abeam, but slow to windward.
3. Although a picturesque and traditional vessel it is impractical for general modern purposes. It is certainly not for a beginner, and can be too expensive for many advanced yachtsmen to run.
4. It allows many masts; up to seven have been used! The idea is that the sails and masts fore are smaller, both becoming progressively larger as one moves aft.

THE LATEEN

1. Probably developed from the Ancient Egyptian Nile craft by way of the Arab *Dhow* (a friend of mine, *Theo von Holst,* sailed on one of them in the Persian Gulf, and found it quite efficient). Still found throughout the Eastern Mediterranean, the Lateen keeps its popularity because of its simplicity and easy handling. The mast is short; the yardarm long.
2. This does not mean that a beginner should take one out to sea, certainly not until proficient on rivers and in quiet estuaries, etc.
3. The sail is hoist on a slanting, long yard, so that the

YAWL

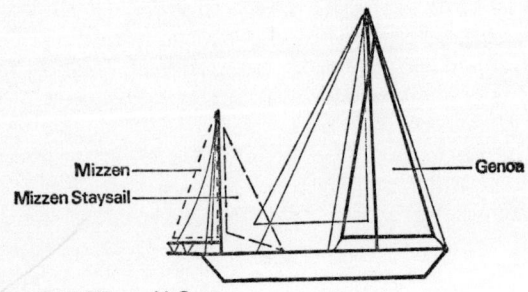

BERMUDAN RIG (a) with Genoa

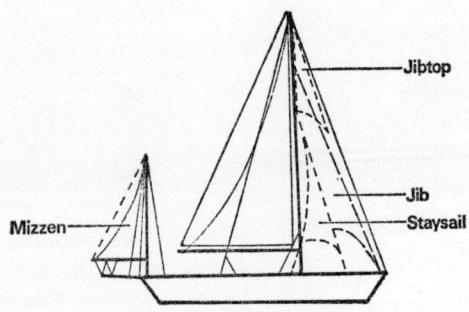

BERMUDAN RIG (b) with Jib, Staysail and Jib Topsail

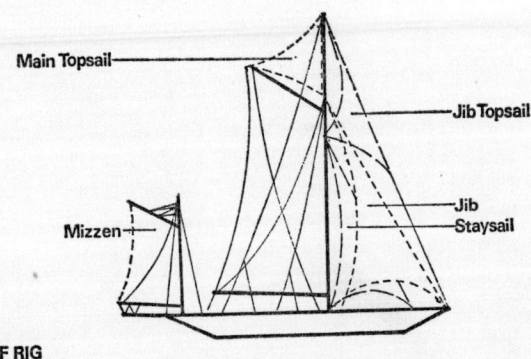

GAFF RIG

THE BEGINNER'S GUIDE TO SAILING

SCHOONER

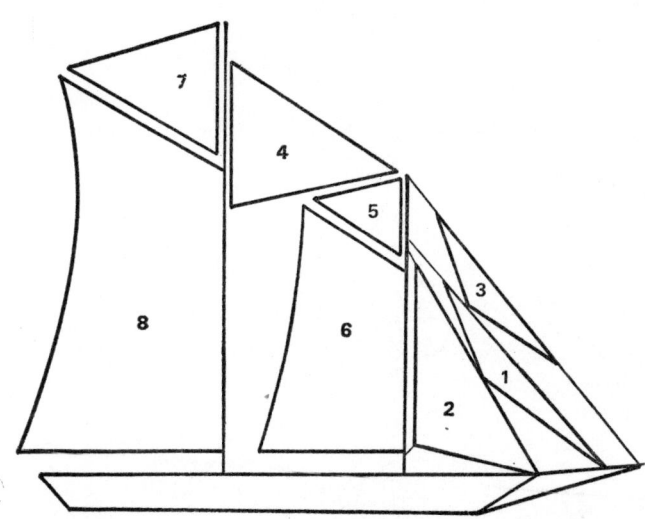

GAFF-RIGGED

1 Jib
2 Staysail
3 Jib Topsail
4 Main Topmast
5 Yankee Topsail
6 Foresail
7 Main Topsail
8 Mainsail

top end of the yard is high above the actual mast, the lower end extends downwards and fore, so that the lateen is the father of the fore-and-aft rig. It is more efficient to windward than it looks.

4. The foot of the sail is held by sheets and not attached to a boom.

THE LUG
1. Still popular with some dinghy sailors. Rarely found in craft over 4 tons.
2. The lug is a four-sided sail with a yardarm, either with or without boom.

LATEEN

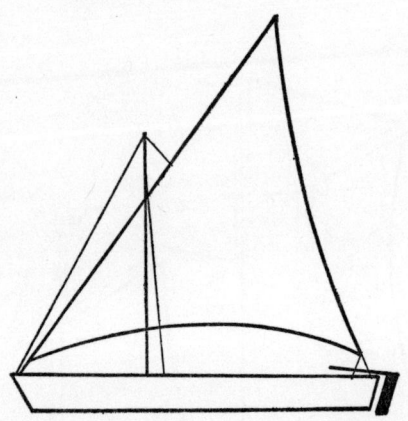

LUG

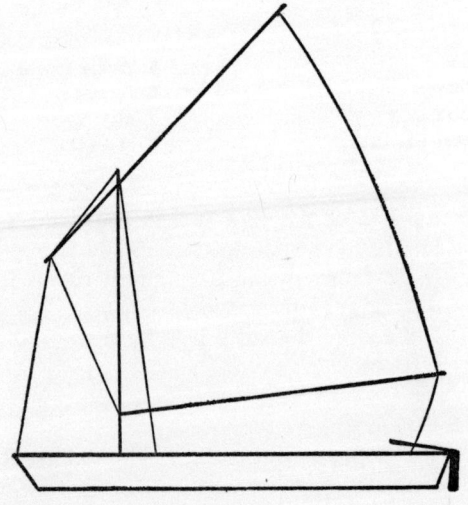

LUG WITH BOOM

3. The boomless lug is called a *standing* lug.
4. The head of the sail bends in to the mast which is fairly short, and usually in a *tabernacle* which houses the foot of the mast, and allows it to be lowered when passing beneath low bridges, entering harbour, etc.
5. The lugsail is not easy to reef or stow.
6. If you are beating to windward the sail may tend to droop to leeward.
7. It can give a beginner a lot of pleasure provided no racing is contemplated. It makes an interesting day cruiser.

THE SPRIT
1. Seen on the old Thames sailing barges, which still celebrate an annual race at Southend, Essex.
2. This is included for historical reasons. It is more a specialist's rig with a spar diagonal to the mainmast to which it is attached at the lower part of the mast. There is no boom nor gaff.
3. Owners of these rare barges love them, and frequently live aboard.

THE FULL BATTENED MAINSAIL
1. When I was a boy I often saw this rig on the *Wester Schelde*, and later at the mouth of the *Elbe* and the *Jadebucht*. But I rarely see it now.
2. Efficient enough for general travelling but slower and clumsier to handle than more modern rigs. Can be used with gaff or gunter.

Several of the boats shown are depicted in Bermuda, Gaff or Gunter rig.

THE BERMUDA has a three cornered (*leg o' mutton*) mainsail. Scientific research confirms that the longer the *luff* (leading edge of a sail; first part to meet the oncoming wind) the greater the driving power developed by it. Therefore the bermuda is a very fast sail to windward.

It is extremely easy to handle, especially by one man. But the bermuda demands a very tall mast, and in rough going

SPRIT

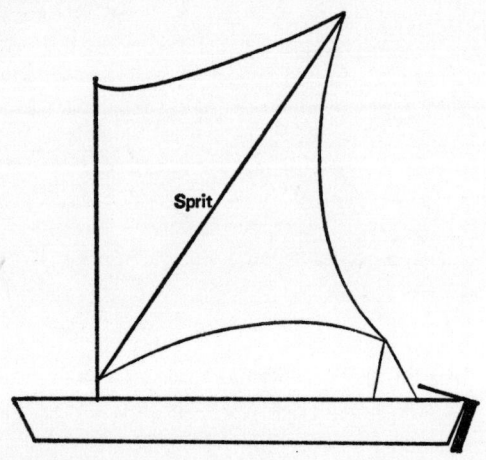

FULL BATTENED MAINSAIL

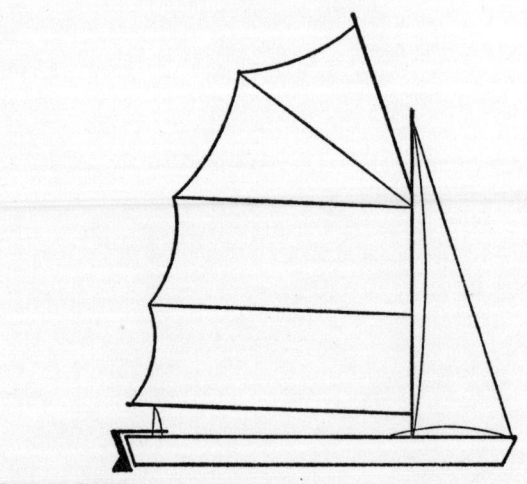

GAFF OR GUNTER

the mast may be damaged by a storm.

A disadvantage is that this sail travels up the mast by means of metal slides along the luff which glide up a track on the mast. Salt, verdigris, and the like can clog the track, making it difficult in a storm to get the sail down (when a gale may tear it) or hoisted, but basically this depends upon whether you check the slide *daily if cruising,* or before and after a voyage on short runs. On a long voyage a man may get tired, exhausted even, so busy about emergencies, cooking etc. that he forgets to attend to this detail, and from such neglect comes the criticism of the bermuda. Also, if the mast gets bent the slide will be inoperative.

It is the most popular rig for ocean racing, and is used by most long-distance yachtsmen. It is easy to gybe with a bermuda.

It is very easy to reef and to handle but not very effective if reefed. It needs only one halyard to hoist it.

Battens (thin strips of wood or plastic) can be inserted into the batten pockets and will keep the sail in an unbroken curve which gives it a better aerodynamic shape.

The sail cannot be hoisted easily if the wind is aft.

It is not very powerful if you are reaching or running.

THE GAFF

This is a square sail. Although not used by many racers it is unlikely to go out of fashion because it has virtues of its own.

It is very much better when driving on a broad reach or running.

It is quick and easy to reef because one simply lowers the peak of the gaff.

It gives a better performance once it is reefed than does a bermuda.

It is easy to lower when the wind is aft, and the old-fashioned hoops *never* jam as do the slides of a bermuda.

It needs two halyards to hoist it. It is clumsier to stow than a bermuda, and is nowhere so good to windward as the bermuda.

The shorter mast is less of a hazard in rough weather.

A BERMUDA MAINSAIL

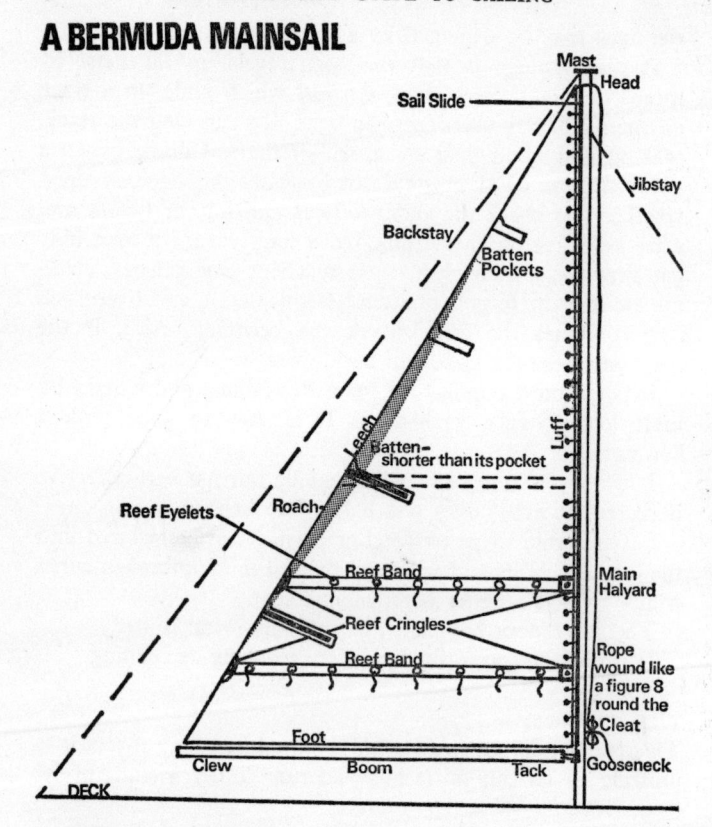

1. STAYS support the mast.
2. GOOSENECK is a metal fitting which is hinged and holds a spar (on which the sail is set) to the mast.
3. BOOM is a spar that stretches out the foot of a sail.
4. To REEF is to shorten (lower) the sail to make a boat easier to handle in rough weather.
5. REEF BAND is a layer of sail cloth to give extra toughness to this part.
6. The dark-shaded area on the leech is the ROACH & is the slightly curved edge.
7. CLEW is where leech and foot meet.
8. TACK is where luff and foot meet.
9. HEADS is where the top of the sail meets the mast.
10. CLEAT enables a rope to be twisted round without being tied. Essential for emergencies. A wet rope never can get knotted or stuck on a cleat.

THE GUNTER

The yard is as long as the boom, maybe longer, is equipped with jaws which clasp the mast at right angles, and is hoisted or lowered by a halyard.

It provides a high, almost bermudan type, aerofoil action on a short mast; it is quickly lowered and easily stowed away. It is useful if you have to pass under low bridges on up-river or canal sailing, but apart from river, canal, lake and estuary sailing, the gunter is not easily adaptable to coastal or deep water sailing.

It is a clumsy rig in rough weather or powerful tidal streams.

SAILS

The mainsail has been dealt with under the headings of bermuda, gaff and gunter, and notes on lateen, lug, fully battened mainsail also apply. The mainsail is the largest on a boat, and is usually amidships where it can be most easily handled.

THE JIB

This cuts down the amount of turbulence formed to the leeward of a mainsail, making it flap unduly (losing wind), for when the jib is hoisted it causes the wind to affect the leeward side of the mainsail. If there is flapping when the jib has been hoisted two alternative reasons are possible:
(a) mainsail old and stretched out of correct shape.
(b) jib is badly trimmed; lower, and hoist again properly.

The jib is the foremost headsail.

THE STAYSAIL

This is a smaller sail set on the stays (which support the mast). The fore staysail is, therefore, a sail which has been set on the fore-stay of the mast (main). Clearly a staysail can be used with every mast the boat has.

A staysail strongly reinforces the effect of the jibsail. Occasionally in squalls a staysail can be used instead of a jib (which is bigger), because there is a limit to the amount of windforce a boat can take while still keeping on course. Too much sail does more harm than too little.

FORESAILS

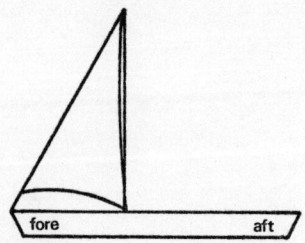

JIB - The foremost headsail

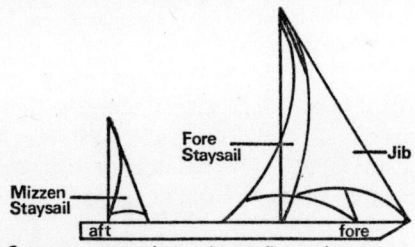

STAYSAIL - Set on any stay and named according to the stay

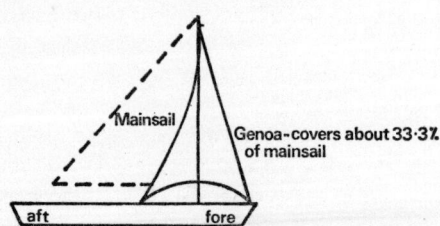

GENOA

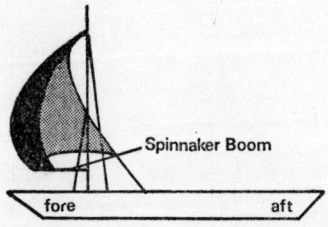

SPINNAKER

THE GENOA

This is basically a jib sail, but one with differences.

It is sheeted in farther aft than is usual for normal jib or foresails.

It is basically a racing sail, much used in sheltered waters or offshore work.

It is usually about one-third the size of the mainsail.

It is at its best on a reach or going to windward, at its worst in tacking.

If sheeted hard it can point closer than almost any other headsail.

It exerts violent pressure on the mast, so backstays must be very strong.

It is not advised for an old hull or weak one. It is sheeted below, not at the masthead. A disadvantage is that if the boat heels the foot of the genoa may sweep the water.

THE SPINNAKER

A controversial sail, used mainly for racing in light weather. Its immediate disadvantage is that it does cut down forward visibility, and for a chap who wants to keep a clear lookout ahead it is a nuisance.

It is a three-cornered foresail, controlled by a sheet, has three clews to secure it, and is held by a spinnaker boom attached to the mast on the opposite side to the mainboom.

At its best it can give remarkable speed, but it is wholly unsuited for a one-man boat (some experts have succeeded, but experts always do—usually in spite of all).

It is powerful for reaching and running, but otherwise a nuisance.

ADDITIONAL NOTES

1. Sail before the mast is technically more efficient than sail carried aft.
2. The lateral driving power of wind on a close-hauled sail is about four times that of the longitudinal force.
3. Even on a ship without sails wind eddies build up around the mast; even people standing on deck have an inter-relationship with the wind currents.

HULL SHAPES

showing rudder & tiller | showing sternpost, tiller & rudder | showing rudder

TRANSOM   **COUNTER**   **CANOE**

STERN SHAPES

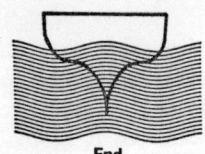 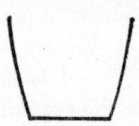 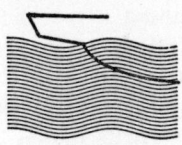

End   Birds eye view   Side

CRUISER

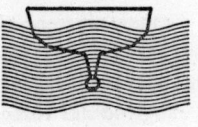  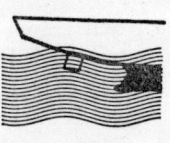

End   Birds eye view   Side

RACER

unching into adventure.

Hoisting sail.

Racing brings out the best in you.

The most exhilarating thrill in the wo

4. The amount of sail carried is in ratio to the number of masts and/or their height.
5. The larger the area of sail carried the more is the angle of heeling (one reason for reducing sail during a storm.
6. The sail which a boat can safely carry is in ratio to the square of her length on the waterline. An ocean-going racer may take 100% but from then on we work downwards.
7. Kenichi Horie found the genoa too unwieldly for solo sailing, particularly because if the mast is forward (sloop etc.) it may be difficult to bring her bows to windward in a storm.

> *Quickly aboard bestow you,*
> *And with a merry gale,*
> *Swell your stretched sayle*
> *With vows as strong*
> *As the winds that blow you*
>
> Michael Drayton
> (*Voyage to the Virginias*)
> (1563-1631).

STERNS

Not only does the rig of a boat tell you something, but the stern is also a guide to performance.

The *Counter* which is the most expensive stern, slams in a rough following sea, but is useful to a racer because it provides untaxed waterline length when heeling. Commonly found with a U-shaped hull.

The *Canoe* stern will take a following sea very well, especially because less water is likely to come aboard. Not so much room below, restricted cabin space.

The *Lifeboat* is similar to the canoe stern, and is fairly good in bad weather.

The *Transom* is at once the cheapest stern to build and the most useful for using on an outboard engine. It has most room below in the cabin. Takes more water on board during

THE BEGINNER'S GUIDE TO SAILING
FINDING YOUR WAY ABOARD SHIP

FORE (go forard)

Stem

Port Bow

Starboard Bow

Fore & Aft Line

Main Mast

Port Beam

Starboard Beam

PORTSIDE→ also LARBOARD

Athwart

←STARBOARD

Mizzen Mast

Port Quarter

Starboard Quarter

Stern

Right Aft

AFT (go aft)

rough weather, and is more easily manipulated by a following sea.

HULLS

The hull needs to provide your boat with a lateral stability that will balance the sails, otherwise the wind would just push a boat sideways and nobody would get anywhere at all.

The object of the hull is also to displace sufficient water to support the entire weight of the boat. Archimedes, 287-212 B.C.) discovered that any floating object displaces its own weight in water.

No single hull can serve all purposes. But a hull is influenced by what you need overall. The deep U shape with greater stability and buoyancy is more logical if you need more accommodation below decks, i.e. if you expect to be living on board for more than a day or weekend. The V shape is more likely to be sought when racing is the first consideration, and comfort last. What we call a U or V shape is, of course only an approximation to these letters and not an exact copy. A long shallow U can be very fast in racing. The length of the boast increases its speed up to certain limits, just as increase of beam decreases speed, again within certain limits. William Froude (1810-79) discovered coefficients of friction which relate the length and frictional resistance ratios to the square of the known speed, so that the effect of the hull creating resistance in wave form on the water could be estimated. The eddies that the path of a boat creates also exercises a retarding force to its forward progress.

If the hull is heeled right over by the wind so that the rails are touching the wave crests, however impressive this looks to the uninitiated it means that the boat is suffering from an increased frictional resistance, and a boat that does this too easily is not a good buy.

You should try for a boat that will not heel whenever she is close-hauled (one that does is called a hardmouthed bitch), nor do you want one that will luff into the eye of the wind as soon as you drop down into the galley for some grub; nor again a boat that will start to yaw before the wind. Hope and pray you get a well-balanced boat that can be trusted to keep

HULLS & RESISTANCE

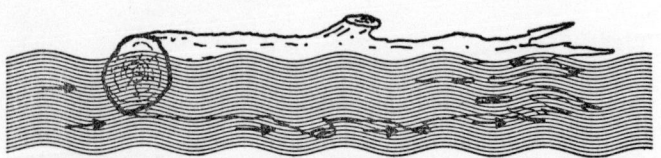

Strong drag caused by uneven multiple surfaces
1 TREE TRUNK

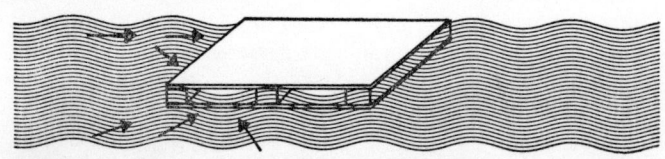

Less drag but difficult to control direction due to width (Beam)
2 RAFT

Reduced resistance
3 INDIAN CANOE

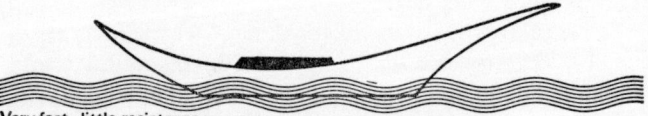

Very fast - little resistance
Note: 'Bowsprit' which developed centuries later on the Clippers
4 ESKIMO ANGMASSALIK KAYAK

on her course without you spending 24 hours a day at the helm.

We have to remember the action of the wind on the sails is only effective as aerofoil force when it utilises to the full the pressure of the water flowing past the hull (hydrofoil force), both turning into energy that forces the boat forwards.

All that glitters is not gold, and all that is advertised as new, progressive and revolutionary contains a lot of the dross of gimmicks. When Sir Francis Chichester was in the Roaring Forties in *Gypsy Moth IV* he wrote: *I would have given a lot to have a good old-fashioned hanks on my sails.* Because the old-fashioned hanks could not jam, and the gales of the Southern latitudes are not the time and place to have to find out the disadvantages that some inventor failed to foresee.

The original Viking craft were of a far superior design to the boats commonly used in the Elizabethan era. Indeed some long-distance Viking long-boats were built with loose planks, held together by leather hinges; thus they flexed with the waves and could not be harmed by them!

For sheer buoyancy the Celtic *curragh*, in which St. Brennan is said to have voyaged to Iceland and beyond, requires a lot of beating, but it is slow. Seaworthiness depends, however, more upon the sailor than his craft. Many Norwegians sailed across to England during the Second World War in craft never designed for anything more than an hour's off-shore trip round the bay.

The illustration *Hulls and Resistance* shows how strong drag forces are built up by uneven multiple surfaces. A raft has less drag (resistance to forward motion) than a log but is difficult to control directionally.

The canoe and the kayak have beautiful lines (see my *Beginner's Guide to Swimming and Water Sports* for more details about canoe movements).

KEELS

Generally speaking, the keel is the significant part of the hull because in the final analysis it is it that enables a boat to move forward (sailing goes on as much below the water as above it). Without a keel a boat can slide to leeward wherever the wind would blow it. So the lower the keel the better the leverage it exerts against heeling. A keel yacht can very rarely capsize, but there is more likelihood of masts being snapped and sails blown away in a storm *if the boat is badly handled*.

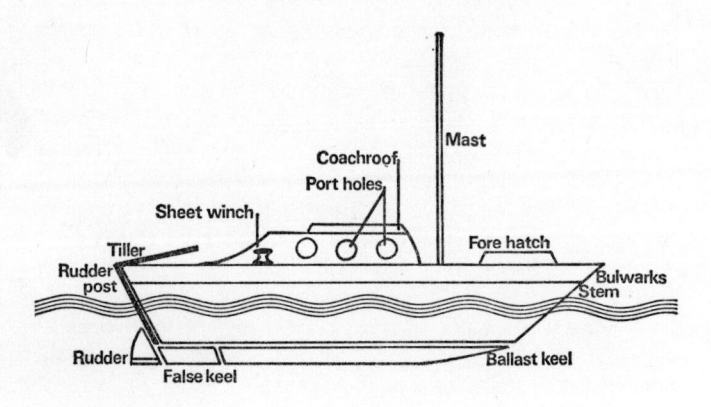

The depth of the keel relates to the amount of leeway a boat makes (all boats make some). From 3-8 tons it is rarely more than 3°, but with a very deep keel it may be as little as 1°.

Some boats use ballast fastened to the bottom of the keel to bring it deeper into the water. Ballast is also placed low down in the hull. Inside ballast consist of iron or lead pigs. But inside ballast, especially if it consists of old chains, etc. has been known to shift in a storm—with unhappy results. *For seagoing yachts outside ballast is advisable for better stability*. Twin bilge keels are suitable for exploring shallow creeks, rivers etc. They also enable a boat to stand upright at low tide in tidal moorings. Their suitability at sea, even for large catamarans, is highly disputed.

Generally speaking, a keel boat is too heavy for lifting without a crane, and this does imply that a permanent mooring is required. I would prefer not to use a twin bilge keel for seagoing myself.

CENTREBOARD

This is a keel that can be lowered or raised as required, and is a compromise between a keel and virtually no keel. It is popular for trailer-born boats. But for this advantage there is a corresponding minus—the centreboard boat can capsize more easily because the keel does not weigh enough to resist strong pressure on the sails.

Make certain that the housing for the centreboard can be easily cleaned with a strip of metal; it is easy for debris, mud and stones to lodge in centreboard housing.

GENERAL

It is widely accepted that the greater the draught the better the performance of the boat to windward.

A self-draining cockpit is essential. A cruiser designed for long distance or weekend voyages should have a keel, but twin bilge keels will suffice for estuarine cruising, shoals and rivers. Avoid a hull with long overhangs if you plan offshore or deep-sea cruising. An outboard rudder is easier to repair, and is better for cruising.

HOW TO DECIDE WHAT YOU WANT TO BUY

In his outstanding book *Kodoku* that remarkable sailor Kenichi Horie wrote: *'If you make up your mind to do something, there is only one way to go about it. Work out your own ideas on the general course you are going to follow and stick to them; stand on those basic ideas and assume responsibility for your actions. You may make mistakes, there may be details in your plan that could have been improved upon by relying upon someone else's advice, but basically it has to be your personal responsibility to conceive and carry out the project.*

With the aid of the information here you should be able to make a little money go a long way.

Firstly, analyse from this chapter exactly what sort of boat you want, put down all the points for and against. What sort of sailing are you after? Mainly cruising or mainly racing? If it is racing be careful not to go in for the wrong class of boat. If you want an auxiliary engine find out what speed limits there are on the rivers etc. you expect to sail upon. In general, a 10 h.p. may be the maximum practical for you. If it is a general run-about boat, check the speed limits, and take more advice from locals than from salesmen who don't know the local waters so well. Think carefully about where you will sail—Rivers and lakes? Estuarine and coastal areas? Seagoing? Then there comes a time factor. How do you intend to use the boat? Day-sailing? Weekends or longer voyages? How social is the boat to be? A haven of rest from the womenfolk and the cares of business? A friend with you to help crew? A family boat?

Do not forget that the size of the boat affects mooring fees, usually charged by the footage of boat. But one thing I advise you to dismiss is the old maxim 'if you want to stand up go on deck'. That may serve for a few racing enthusiasts, but get in a really cramped boat during a Force 7 blow, and you may regret the lack of space.

Few people are unbiased with regard to their boats. Talk to several before accepting their enthusiasms about their particular type of boats. Don't forget that the enthusiast you were talking to may have double your income, and can afford overhauls and repairs that could bankrupt you. Go slow! Secondly, analyse what materials you want the boat to be built of. It saves you time and money looking if you know what you are looking for. Metal is ostensibly durable. But look what happens to some cars. Rust cannot be seen until suddenly, one day a plate stoves in, and maybe, if you are afloat, the water follows in too. The creeping chemical action of rust is a curse. I think that emergency repairs to metal by an amateur are more difficult than to other materials. Against this, many metal-built boats still in service are 100 years old or more. Wood, man's oldest and truest boat-building material, is easier to repair in an emergency, and one need have no fear of marine ply so long as it conforms to B.S.1088. Care must be taken about what metals come in contact with the wood. Some corrode more easily than others and affect the wood too: Brass is best. Glassfibre and plastic resin-built boats are the most popular. They are slightly more expensive, but are easier to clean, need little servicing, and are surprisingly strong. Some have crashed on to rocks without showing a single hairline crack, and with no damage at all. Some anti-fouling may be needed, but many plastics don't require this.

Catalogues and adverts speak of GRP, which means Glass Reinforced Plastic. A boat with balsa or foam inside the GRP will have added buoyancy and will be slightly stronger. Epoxy resins are held to be superior to polyester resin, but cost more.

Wood is, of course, warmer to look at and live with than the cold colours of GRP, so some manufacturers coat the inside of the cabins with carpetting or wood panelling—according to how much money you can spend.

The chief advantage of GRP and other plastics is the fact that you can leave them afloat during the winter months, whereas wood is often better if hauled ashore (even then too much drying out is bad for the wood).

COSTS

The price of the boat is not the entire cost to you. There are probably delivery charges, unless you buy it already afloat or near your moorings. Ah, yes, then like a car there must be somewhere to keep it if it is too big to haul on a trailer behind your car. This place is called the mooring, and clubs or people owning moorings charge you, usually per foot-length of the boat, either monthly or yearly. Many owners of moorings live by the shore and can keep a friendly eye on your property for you, so never begrudge what you pay for your moorings. There may well be a club membership fee to pay, and you should, if it is a second-hand boat, make an estimate to cover possible alterations, repairs, etc. If there is any chance of taking the boat into foreign waters you should have it properly registered. This makes it easier for the insurance and customs people you deal with.

Now, beginners do not always realise that buying a boat does not *always* mean you have got a boat ready to sail. Many British boatbuilders, thank heavens, are delivering a boat ready to sail away to Tahiti or Timbukto as your fancy pleases, but some do not supply *sails*, anchors, or other *essential equipment*. Particularly when buying a second-hand boat it is imperative that you check the *inventory*; that is the list of things it has aboard.

The inventory will obviously vary for racing and cruising,

but a club, salesmen or local sailors will advise you about what you require.

Apart from the sails, sheets, halyards, and the like you will need an anchor, say a 20 lb. CQR, about 25 fathoms of chain, some warps, a hand anchor winch, a compass in gimbals, one bilge pump (preferably two) a sink, two water carriers about five gallons each, a distance log, two fire extinguishers. A dinghy or inflatable is advisable if you are doing offshore, estuarine or deep sea cruising. You need sail stowage bags, anchor light, both port and starboard navigational lights, a searchlight might also be useful during a fog or late at night. Fenders, a boathook and some personal buoyancy jackets should also be carried.

You can have either a marine toilet with pump(s); make sure they work properly; Check that the valve to empty it into the sea shuts easily and firmly; Or you can have a chemical toilet bucket; these are quite efficient and clean, and they don't let seawater into the boat.

With respect to cooking, you should definitely have gimbals, you don't get any help from a cooker that is sliding all over the galley during a storm. Of the alternatives alcohol (methylated spirits) cookers are very expensive to use. I think paraffin is too dangerous, unless you know your boat can stop still without pitching and rolling while you cook. Electricity is good for cooking if the boat's generator can stand up to it.

This leaves us with but one good alternative, bottled gas. I began using this when I lived on a boat in Stockholm, I found it cheap, clean, very fast and most efficient.

Bottled gas is heavier than air, so it can sink, even down to the bilges. If it is allowed to escape one carelessly-lit match could sink your boat without trace. It is possible to install the cooker and the bottles of gas so carefully that no movement or damage can take place, but there is no substitute for being careful.

The inventory starts there, and can end where you like, but don't forget spare sails, just in case those you're using get ripped in a force 10 wind. For those whose nagivation is like the bellman in Lewis Carroll's *Hunting of the Snark*, it might be as well to take a large bell on board too.

DO YOUR MOORINGS GOVERN WHAT BOAT YOU OWN

Well, yes, because if you have a mooring in the upper reaches of a tidal river you may find that the ocean-going racer (1910 vintage) with that deep keel you bought cannot get there even during flood tide!

There are three types of mooring: *Afloat* (both ebb and flood tide) sea or river. *Aground* during ebb tides, and the mooring you should avoid like the plague—*Mud*—way up a creek, with a chance of getting off at Spring or Autumn tides! If you go to buy a second-hand boat on such a mooring, make it a condition of sale that the seller delivers the boat to you (if he can move it himself).

TRAILERS

If you get a boat which can be transported overland, behind a car, make sure the car is powerful enough to haul the trailer: Check with the manufacturer of the car, not the seller of the trailer.

Most modern trailers are constructed so that they can be driven to the very edge of the water, then shoved off into the surf, whence the boat can be floated off into deep water, and gentled back on again (ah, the joy of a centreboard!). You will find that a winch and pulleys take the strain out of manhandling a boat.

Generally speaking, you must allow about another three feet under the depth of the keel before your boat will float safely into the waves, although there is nothing to stop a few of you wading in to pull her out (centreboard up, please).

Do check with your local police what regulations exist about trailing a boat, speed limits, and any special requirements about brakes, and what lights must be shown when trailing.

SECOND-HAND BOATS

Unless, like Lear's *Jumblies*, your head is green and your hands are blue, don't go to sea in a sieve. Many second-hand boats are good, many are sieves just waiting to let the water in. There is one sure way of finding out. You must have a proper survey carried out by a really good surveyor if you plan to go to sea or sail in coastal waters or estuaries. If it is just on a fairly good stretch of river, and if you can swim well, you might be justified in taking a risk. I wouldn't. If you buy a second-hand yacht and ask somebody to deliver her to you it is then *your* responsibility to ascertain that she is safe to sail. You have no right to ask a man to risk his life in a boat that is not properly equipped, and the boat must be insured by you from the moment it sets sail to reach your moorings.

Unless you have really reliable and knowledgeable friends you had best employ the services of a yacht broker. He will charge 10% of the purchase price (usually) for his services, but he will *save you a lot of money and time*. He will find you the sort of boat you are looking for, or perhaps as near as makes no difference; he is in touch with other yacht brokers all over the country, and he will not recommend a boat that is not sound (that is to save his business reputation as much as to look after your interests). You must be fair to him, and, using this book's advice, sort out what type of a boat you want, and tell him what price range interests you, and stress the maximum figure (inclusive) you can afford to pay, and make clear it is the maximum. The more precise you are the more quickly he can help you.

WHAT YOU MUST KNOW

Adverts for second-hand and new boats contain a lot of abbreviations. These are the most common:

LOA — length of boat overall.
LWL — length of the boat on the line where she floats in the water.
B — beam.
D — draught.

Measurements are usually given in this order: LOA. LWL. B. D. e.g.: 32 x 25 x 10 x 3'6".

MFV — motor fishing vessel (Suitable sometimes for conversions).
MTB — retired motor torpedo boat (Suitable sometimes for conversions).

TSDY — twin screw diesel yacht.
SSDY — single screw diesel yacht.
TSMY — twin screw motor yacht.
TSDC — twin screw diesel cruiser.

The cheapest time of year to buy a yacht is when the season has come to a close. Often many have been hauled out by then, and you can see more than when the craft is afloat.

To choose one boat you'll need to see two score at least!

Never hurry a decision; if you are told that others are queueing up to buy the boat you are interested in, don't be selfish; let them take the risk; *all* second-hand boats have some possible risk.

If the seller tells you not to bother about a survey because he has a report from a surveyor dated 6 or 12 months ago, think carefully; you might risk it, on the other hand the boat could have been to the Arctic or round Cape Horn in that time. You must decide for yourself, trust to instinct, nothing else will help you. If the vendor is obviously hedging to avoid a survey, forget it, however nice the craft looks, something is dead wrong.

Do not get angry if the broker sends you a list of boats to view which do not match your specifications exactly. He knows that, but wonders whether you might not do as well with some of these he sends you details of, and with a few modifications it could perhaps save you money. Brokers usually know boats better than car salesmen know cars, and they have a good idea about what makes a reasonable compromise. A good idea is to get a friend with a boat to spend a weekend afloat, taking you round some boatyards, many of which are not easily accessible by car (why are boat-yards and clubs so often at the bottom of a lane that is little better than a quagmire?).

Yachts are sometimes quoted in tonnage. The idea started when the number of wine casks (*tuns* to you) a boat could carry was the basic measurement. About a century ago the Thames tonnage was introduced, and this is based upon a simple mathematical formula. L—length. B—beam.

$$\frac{\text{L–B} \times \text{B}^2}{188} \left\{ \text{e.g.:} \quad \frac{32\text{–}8 \times 64}{188} \quad \ldots 8 \text{ tons.} \right\}$$

Whereas a car and a caravan tend to deteriorate with age this is not necessarily true of a boat. Even metal boats, if properly coated with zinc, can last decades without showing signs of age.

You should always look for any obvious distortion in the external lines of a boat, particularly the curvature; this usually indicates storm damage. Examine the sails; if they are frayed or chafed maybe the whole boat has been neglected.

An old boat that has been newly painted *all over* probably has something to hide. Boat owners selling their craft are not usually so kindhearted as to do so much work for somebody else. If there is any discoloration of paint, or bubbles in its surface, then the wood below is certainly rotten.

If possible, try to get the broker or surveyor to come with you to see your intended purchase, and don't begrudge him his fee if he says 'don't' or just curls up into a ball of laughter. He has saved your life!

If you want a cabin cruiser remember to check that there is decent headroom and sufficient berths. Avoid berths that are athwart ships (getting rarer nowadays) because although the fore and aft pitching is not disturbing to a sleeper, the side to side rolling makes sleep almost impossible. There has to be an engine, preferably inboard, if you plan to go to deep waters. Is it easily accessible? You always need some locker where oilies can be hung to drip-dry, and if the craft has a shower cabinet with the W.C. this is ideal—provided it still leaves room for you! Is there room for sails and cables to be stowed? Do the hatches batten down tightly? Is there space to sleep in, cook in, keep and plot charts in?

Like W. S. Gilbert's *Ruler of the Queen's Navee* certain boat salesmen *never go to sea*. Do not be too confiding and trusting in their words. Whatever they assure you, don't buy a shoal draft centreboard craft for deep water work. A centreboard with ballast keel is safer for coastal trips. Glamorous as it is to possess an old ocean racer (perhaps she won cups in her day) remember she is bound to heel and your voyages will be more wet than dry. An old racer never makes a good cruiser.

If the broker brightly suggests you should look at a converted MFV, remember it is usually uncommonly roomy below, will sail well, be rather slow, most likely have very good stability, but watch for structural deterioration inside.

A 50/50 motor sailer never sails so fast as pure sail. The hull lines and propeller slow her down. When you use the motor alone the mast catches windage; so does the rigging; this slows down the effect of motor without masts, etc. You can never get 100% advantage in boats. But these craft are very useful for the more mature citizen who needs to hurry back after a delightful day's sailing, maybe for social or business reasons.

The lower the profile of the boat the less the effect of a violent storm will be. The higher the area above actual deck level the more there is for rough weather to work upon, but this depends, of course, upon whether you expect to be out in unsheltered waters in bad weather.* Catamarans and Trimarans are specialised sailing craft, I shall not say much about them. They need larger moorings, beamwise; cats are usually self-righting in a capsize. Cats are fairly strong in bad weather; they have stability and speed more in ratio to your sailing experience and sea conditions. I don't think they are suitable for a first boat. Although many men with excellent sailing experience have voyaged in lesser boats I wouldn't like to go to sea in a boat less than 25 ft. for cruising, and a long voyage needs at least 33 ft. For an ocean passage you need 42 ft. But after that you need a crew of a least two to handle her, and tough work it will be for both of you. Boats below 25 ft. seldom have full standing room below decks. Remember if the LWL is 32 ft. the actual cabin space below may well be 10 ft. less than that; ships curve, and not all the curved space is suitable for accommodation. Pinched ends and a wide beam in ratio to LOA is a sure sign that the boat will heel easily.

---

* Beware of amateur conversion jobs, they may have made the craft top heavy.

NOTES

One man who is fairly competent can handle a 35 ft. boat and about 1,000 square foot of sail. Some men have handled much more, but they were far beyond average competence.

An average craft of 25 ft. with a 10 h.p. engine can run about 8 knots; with a 15 h.p. she will reach about 12 knots in calm weather.

If you change a boat's engine for a bigger, more powerful, one remember that you will certainly need a bigger and stronger propeller too, but the larger the propeller the more the drag it causes when sailing without engines.

Moorings, Anchors and the like

1. LEAVING FOR A SAIL

You are standing on the shore. Your newly-bought boat lies at her moorings where the mariner who delivered her left her. How do you get out to your boat? First, don't wade out unless you know the ground very well, and then only with caution, in an emergency. There are many idiots in this world who think it is fun to throw pieces of sharp, rusty metal into a harbour, or on the bed of a river. These often sink in the mud, waiting for some unwary person to step on them, cut himself, and poison his leg. I know of one case which happened only a short while ago.

Wait for the tide and go out by dinghy, inflatable, tender, whatever is available. Occasionally the mud is firm enough for planks to be laid across it; in this case it is often difficult to get your boat afloat. The general rule is—first get water before you try to sail away. The small boats mentioned can either be rowed out, sculled or used with a small outboard engine.

Never leave your engine on the transom. Some light-fingered lads are strong enough to carry it away with them!

Well, now you have got to your boat, you clamber aboard. What do you do with the small rowboat or so that brought you there? Send mother-in-law or some aunt back to shore with it? Try either of the following:

1. Moor it by painter to a link of the yacht's mooring chain. Take care to do this slowly so that you do not entangle it with any of the cordage or chains on your boat. Should you accidentally entangle ropes, chains, and the like, when you attempt to hoist sail and away, instead of gracefully exiting, the tangle will cause you to whizz round in a circle, which is very funny for those watching you from the shore, provided you do not damage their boats in the process.

2. Alternatively you can haul it on deck—very nice if your yacht runs to davits, winches, pulleys etc. Otherwise a bit of strong-arm muscle is needed. It must be lashed down

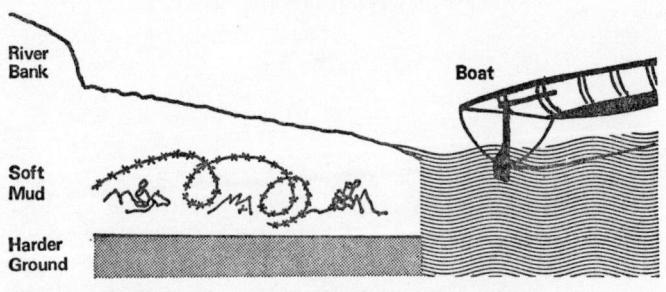

Soft mud is usually full of rusty metal, barbed wire, broken glass etc.

on deck, for if you leave it loose it could become a *lethal* weapon of destruction, crashing about on deck in the smoothest seas. If you are on a normal pleasure cruise you would lash it down keel uppermost. If, however, you have reached the stage where you are going round the world, have run out of water, are waiting desperately for some rain to drink, there would be justification in lashing it in position, keel bottommost.

3. You can tow a boat behind you if you wish. But it will act as a drag; it slows down your forward speed considerably. In so far that it may, under stormy circumstances, crash constantly into your transom or quarters (doing damage to rudder, tiller or planking), it is a confounded, noisy nuisance. There are some occasions when this is justified, but your experience alone will explain this to you, because it depends mostly upon your boat, you and the prevailing weather.

When you cast off, having hoisted sails and carried out all preparations (explained elsewhere), be sure that you don't collide with the tender or runabout you have just moored.

The *exact moment to let go of the mooring chain/cable* is when your mainsail fills with wind, unless you have to leave under a foresail alone. See below: Always leave from a windward shore if possible. It is so much easier. If the tide comes one way, and the wind the other, then it is practical to leave under foresail alone (jib). Only hoist your mainsail when it is obvious that you are free from possible collision with other craft at their moorings down the river, estuary, etc. This leaves you free to turn up into the wind as you need.

GENERAL PLAN FOR COMING IN & MOORING

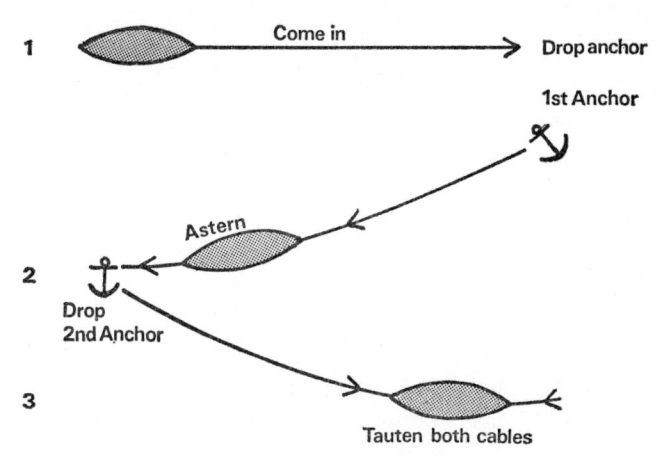

1 Come in → Drop anchor

1st Anchor

2 Astern ← Drop 2nd Anchor

3 Tauten both cables

Ship more or less central between 1st and 2nd Anchors

> *Behind us in our paths we cast*
> *The broken potsheards of the past,*
> (Longfellow)

As you cast off for the very first time you will know what is meant by that song Louis Armstrong sang: *We have all the Time in the world*. For this is what sailing feels like.

1. Don't sail from a lee shore if you can find some way to go from windward.
2. Don't sail to windward with the rudder in the up position; it will strain the rudder fittings.
3. Never have the mainsail hauled tight when you cast off or she may run aground before she has gathered way.

2. COMING BACK TO MOORINGS
   1. Whenever you approach any mooring watch how other craft are lying at anchorage. This shows you where a safe channel is, acts as a guide to the depth of the water (for anchor cable, etc.).
   2. When entering an unknown harbour *read the chart/pilot*

book before you go in, not while entering it. *While* is too late.

3. If anchoring in unknown or unmarked waters use a lead-line to get a reading.
4. In waters which you know but do not use regularly, as well as in unknown harbours, *check with your pilot book* (if available). Often these not only provide details but also photographic instructions on how to enter at different states of the tides.
5. The ideal mooring is one that is protected from the prevailing winds. This simple precaution can save your boat from unnecessary buffeting and damage: If you can choose, take the lee side of a quay.
6. If in tidal waters, you should try to head into the tide as you glide to your chosen mooring, jetty, etc.
7. One of the first things to learn about your craft is how far and how fast she will travel after the sails have been lowered. Experience is the only way of learning this basic essential of mooring.
8. In high winds one may glide in on a bare mast. Even reduced sail area may cause a collision. *Don't lower a sail which is full of wind.*
9. The aim is to come in so that you keep way gently. Too fast is very likely to lose you the mooring buoy.
10. Moving up to windward of your buoy and just drifting down on to it is not wholly reliable, although widely practised.
11. Keep a sharp look out for old mooring chains or buoys in any crowded moorings; it is cheaper than fouling your anchor.
12. If your anchorage or mooring is in deep water, tack up to it. Lower speed by easing the sheets gently, and remember to turn her head into the wind to pick up the mooring buoy.
13. In tidal waters the anchor should be in line with the direction of the tide. The heaviest anchor in line to take the heaviest strain.
14. As you come in, have a boathook at the ready to steady yourself alongside. Have you got the old tyres or rope shock-absorbers in place? If you didn't put them on

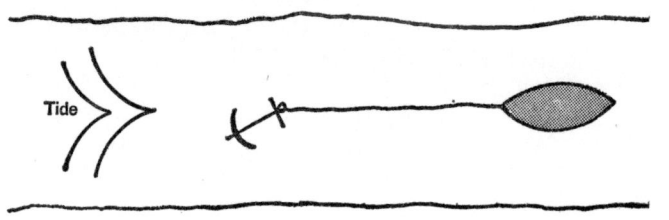

a ESTUARY TIDE

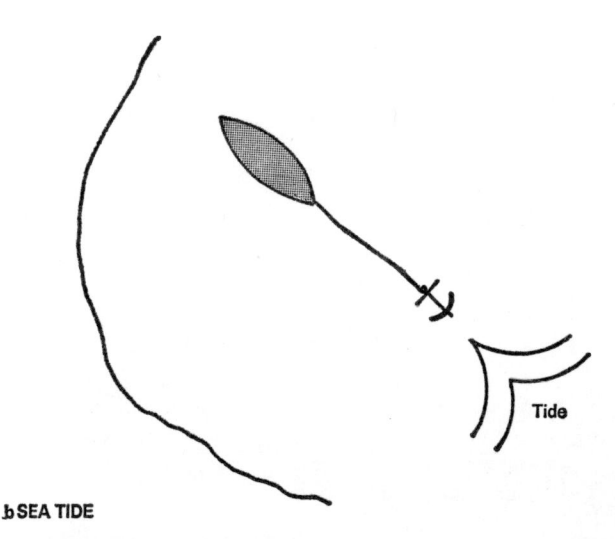

b SEA TIDE

you will certainly remember it the next time. Fenders save years for your boat.

15. Have the anchor ready to go, with sufficient fathoms of cable (estimated or known) allowed for; there must be an adequate allowance for drift, three or four times the actual depth of high tide, but not so much as might cause a collision with other craft at moorings.
16. Remember that a craft moored with only one anchor can be swept round by the tide as it turns, this would foul the anchor and cause her to drag it.
17. One of the drawbacks of learning to sail with a small

dinghy is that, being extremely easy to manoeuvre, they have no problems in mooring.

Practice in mooring is wise; it is always easy when, as Virgil says, *Neptune, in his light chariot glides along the surface of the waves,* but in rougher weather it is only the experienced hand who can moor easily.

18. *Wind and tide the same way*: (Running in).
    (i) Lower mainsail, come in with jib or foresail.
    (ii) Judging distance carefully, lower jib (foresail) before approaching moorings.
    (iii) Drop anchor, snub your cable and check the tidal drift.

19. *Wind against tide*: (Running in).
    (i) Lower mainsail, come in with jib or forestaysail.
    (ii) Judging distance carefully, lower jib or foresail before approaching mooring.
    (iii) Allow her to drift round stern first, drop anchor, etc.

20. *No tide at all* or *wind and tide the same way*: (Close-hauled).
    (i) Luff.
    (ii) Lower jib or foresail.
    (iii) Allow her to drift round stern first, drop anchor, etc.

21. *If wind drops* or *in stays* tack to avoid collision with moored craft.

22. *To leeward and in shallows*:
    (i) Tack carefully.
    (ii) Sails down.
    (iii) Slow and easy, use boathook.
    (iv) If possible have someone in the bows to avoid shallows by pole.

23. *Wind on her beam*: see illustration opposite.

24. Dinghies and centreboard craft ride more with the wind. Keelboats ride more with the tide.

25. *When at mooring or anchorage*:
    Never stow sails that are wet.
    Always dry sail whenever possible.

    Remove battens, stow sail, coil or stow halyards and sheets, only if planning a long stopover.

WIND ON HER BEAM

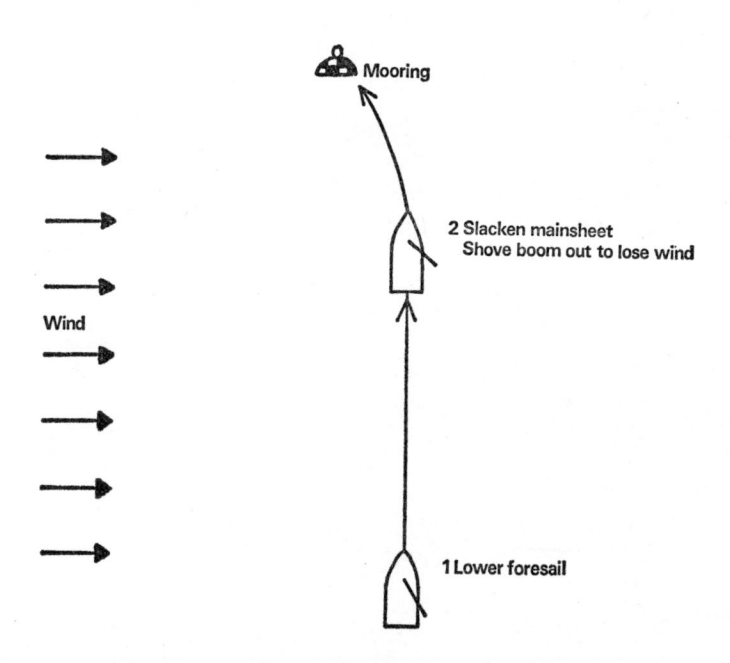

2 Slacken mainsheet
Shove boom out to lose wind

Wind

1 Lower foresail

Mooring

Clean up on deck and below.
Let your ship be as proud of you as you of her.
Do hoist an anchor light to forestay by jib halyard if traffic and common sense recommend it.
Strictly speaking anchoring is with one anchor in use, mooring is with two.

DO
1. Check whether tide is rising or falling, especially if this is a short-term mooring.
2. Do raise centreboard and rudder as you approach the shallows, if you do this before necessary the boat will drift to leeward. Practice makes perfect.
3. Do be sure the cable chain or warp is long enough for the anchor to hold well. A short warp never holds as well as a long warp.

4. Control the movement of the anchor chain, etc. Stand on it if you have no winch (hope you have good balance).
5. Drift the boat on to her trolley if you are trailing her, never drag her over sand, stones or mud.

DON'T
1. Sail on to beach or shore headlong like a viking raider—unless you wish to contribute to the boatbuilder's bank account.
2. Let cable or chain tangle itself up with other gear, it causes collisions and loss of time.
3. Throw in anchor cables or chain as you have seen some hero in a pirate film do; it can ruin centreboard or keel, propeller, rudder and foul your own anchor.
4. Care what friends in the yacht club think, just do what is right; however awkward it may look to somebody watching, they'll not pay for your new boat!
5. Don't stand up unnecessarily in a high wind, it is often advisable to lie face down head over the bows to pick up a buoy.
6. Lower mainsail if wind behind you is strong and the sail full out, it could tear the sail—very expensive!

ENGINES
(i) Cut engines about 6 boatlengths from the shore (mooring, jetty, etc.).
(ii) Gently pull lever back astern. As most screws are right turn they pull the bows to starboard.
(iii) Have your boathook ready.

LONG TERM MOORINGS AT HARBOUR WALL ETC.
(The better you can cast a rope ashore the easier it is!)
See the illustration on the opposite page.

ROWING A BOAT AT SEA
The technique is necessarily different to that which one learns for a river, lake or canal, because of the movement of the waves.

Do not tighten your thumb round the oars; that can cause cramp, especially if you are not practised in rowing. Nor do you want to make the arms take the strain of the mighty

LONG TERM MOORINGS

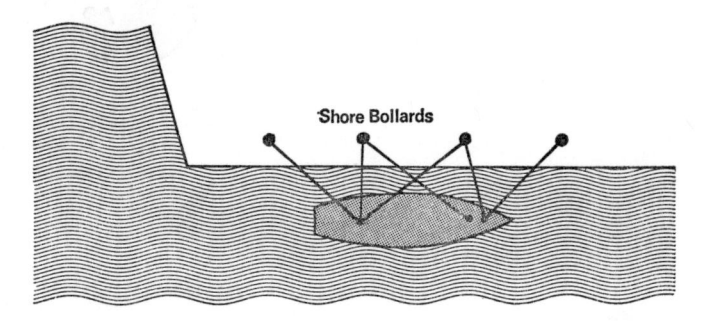

Shore Bollards

pull; the momentum of your entire body is better taking the strain, especially in a rough or choppy sea.

For rowing at sea you normally take shorter, deeper pulls on the oar than you would on calm water, and don't feather your oars, such artistic refinements are best left for the long sweeps back during a race or rowing cruise on a hot summer's afternoon up a somnolent creek. If there were a stiffish wind across the water some feathering might reduce wind resistance created by the oars.

You would normally approach a yacht (or other craft) at about 45° (see illustration p. 58), do not come alongside parallel or the wind will most likely make it difficult for you to steady her and stop.

For reasons lost in antiquity one always seems to bring a rowboat in starboard to a ship's portside.

The middle of a rowboat is the safest place for passengers to leave by, and what part of the yacht you tie up at should be decided by where there is a rope ladder or something similar.

HOW TO HOIST A SAIL

For simplicity's sake I imagine you are starting with a Bermudan mainsail boat.

Attached to the main mast is a main halyard; you use a shackle to fasten this to the head of the sail.

Most modern sails have on the luff grommets which are

ROWING OUT

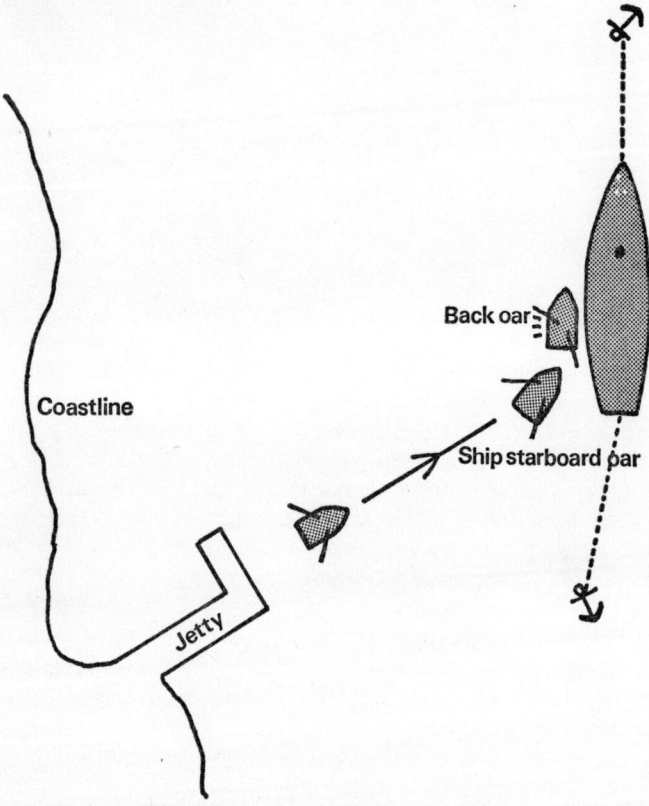

[Diagram labels: Coastline, Jetty, Back oar, Ship starboard oar]

attached to slides; these move neatly up a track on the mast. There is no more to it than that (Sir Francis Chichester, in *Gypsy Moth IV*, found that in the gales of the roaring forties the slides stuck too easily due to salt corrosion in the mast grooves, etc. That is unlikely to happen on short cruises).

A modern ship will have a similar groove for slides along its boom, others may need tying down.

As the sail is fastened, put the battens in the batten pockets, hoist away, and there she is raring to go.

The old English word *bend* originally meant to fasten something to something else, hence *bend the sails* is still

THE BEGINNER'S GUIDE TO SAILING 59

HOME TO A LEE MOORING

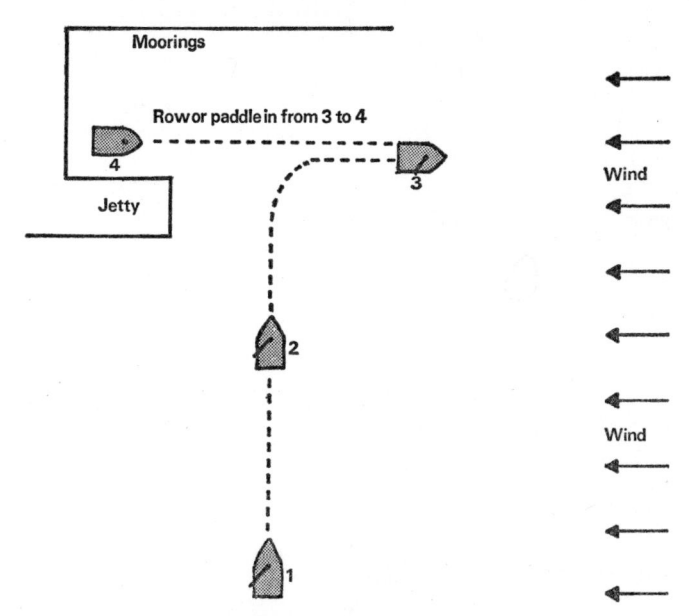

commonly used in nautical circles.

The jib is bent on by twisting or fastening hooks on to the forestay, but you usually begin with the tack end of the jibsail; then the shackles are fastened, the sail is hoisted, you are all ready to go.

Any explanation in words makes this sound a complicated procedure; once, and once only is usually enough for anybody to learn to do it competently for the rest of their lives. When the sheets, halyards, shackles and sails are there in front of your eyes it will all seem so logical that you will feel you knew it all your life—part of the racial subconscious as the psychologist Jung would have said.

Do remember to get the luff as straight as possible, then you follow the directions for leaving moorings.

If you have a trailer boat and need to erect the mast on each occasion do get the supplier to demonstrate this manoeuvre several times *before* you part with the cash.

Make sure that you keep the upper part of the coiled halyard pointing *upwards* when you lift it off the cleat to lower sail (which is your nearest equivalent to the brakes on a car); that is one time when you don't want to risk carelessly coiled and ravelled rope.

Be sure that when you fasten a halyard to a cleat you do not let go of the rope so that the luff of the sail slackens.

If in doubt never be too proud to ask for help; every mooring I have known has been full of people only too ready to help. Many unattached lads will give you a lot of help joyfully if you offer to take them along with you; they may know a lot more than you do but cannot afford a boat of their own. Take one along if you need a bit of help, give him a sail, and learn something in return.

LAUNCHING FROM A LEEWARD SHORE

For the purposes of the discussion we assume the wind is blowing at a nice 90° on to the shore from which you want to launch your boat. One brave crewman must be tough enough to go into the water and hold your boat to the wind while the luckier partner hoists the sail (if you go regularly from a leeward shore, take it in turns). And do let the rudder down gently as soon as the shelving bottom will enable you to do so.

If you are trailing a boat, it might be wiser to seek out a launching place which is at sufficient angle to the oncoming wind to avoid the difficulty (particularly if you are solo).

Don't foget to allow for the fact that a smaller angle than 45° is not very practical if you're closehauled.

As for returning to a leeward shore, it is often safer, if not essential to paddle, punt or row backward to the jetty or mooring. (See illustration p. 59.)

If you were riding out at a mooring offshore you would let a contrary wind and tide situation drift you sternwards until clear of neighbouring boats when you can hoist sail without fear of collision.

Take your time to get out of a tight mooring, don't rely on your fenders or those of the other fellow to keep you free from damage.

Dinghies and Racing

The dinghy is the most ubiquitous of boats. Many owners use them for a bit of offshore cruising but far more race them, and I deal with them in connection with racing. For many the first taste of sailing comes in a friend's dinghy, gazing in tranced state at the sunshine's diamonds sparkling on the blue-green waves when, in Longfellow's words:
With a sound of sleep the water rippled on the beach below.

THE DINGHY
1. Has a shallow keel, which makes it more difficult to point into the wind.
2. Is very fast, but sacrifices stability to speed more than other yachts; it requires that the crew shift their weight (holding on by toe straps, etc.) to keep stability.
3. Good seamanship is more essential for dinghy sailing than for cruising with a larger boat, because the dinghy is quicker to react to the slightest movement of wind and tide.
4. Its manoeuvrability makes picking up or leaving a mooring deceptively easy.
5. Has about 60 different design classes, corresponding to the variations and needs of different localities, some which are suitable for lake and river being less suitable for coastal work, etc. Advice about different classes is always available from yachting associations, clubs, etc.
6. Owes its popularity to the emergence of marine-ply, synthetic resin glues, etc. Horie sailed the North Pacific in a boat of marine ply $\frac{1}{3}''$ thick.
    The introduction of polyester resins provided small craft with low friction, great tensile strength, relatively little weight, and required scant maintenance.
7. There is one serious warning: When manhandling your dinghy into the water *never* grasp the stays to climb aboard or to lift her by.
8. Reefing can damage (by undue stretching) the racing

sails which are very expensive, so it is essential not to crease or wrinkle them if you are reefing; this applies especially to roller reefing.

RACING

The most voluminous and contentious side of sailing literature is concerned with racing. This section gives some general ideas, tips, and an overall conception of the rules.

1. Boats are classified as being of National or International class, showing which type of competition the *boat* is suitable for.
2. When racing do use a dark burgee; this is more easily seen in glaring sunlight. Racing requires much more attention to the burgee than cruising.
3. If winning is the only goal you have in mind, forget it, this is not for you; in few sports is it so essential *how* you win rather than whether you do.
4. Racing demands sportsmanship as well as seamanship. It teaches you how much seamanship you know; unless there is strict fair play you will miss much of the excitement.
5. If you go into a chandler's and ask for the rules of racing you will probably leave with three to four volumes of some classic work. So, unless you want to become an international authority on the subject, leave that alone for the moment. Rules vary from place to place and race to race.
6. Roughly speaking, races are divided up as follows: Cruising-transoceanic; One-design class (in which every competitor is of the same design); Individual Challenges (one yacht versus another, usually any design); Team races (more of one team to pass the finishing line than of the other team); Special Dinghy races (various classes too); Handicap races.

And so on most sunny weekends it is possible to see enthusiasts, *like Ahab driving the Pequod on to its doom in search of the white whale* (Melville's *Moby Dick*).

The following is a simple summary of the universally-applied rules.

THE BEGINNER'S GUIDE TO SAILING

(a) A boat with wind blowing on her starboard, with main boom on her port, has the right-of-way over a boat with wind port side (boom to starboard).

(b) When two boats are on the same tack, the one to windward keeps clear of that which is to leeward.

(c) In overtaking you must keep clear of the boat being overtaken.

(d) If two or more craft approach a mark on the course those on the outside should yield and let the boat on the inside have water room to sail round first.

(e) If any boat, during a race, hails you for water to tack in this must be yielded.

(f) Whereas most boats not competing will keep out of the way of a race, one may approach racing craft; *the normal rules of right of way will then apply;* a racing pennant gives no exception to this. The straying boat might be in the hands of children, a sick man, etc.

(g) If a competitor deliberately fouls you, and loses you the race, you may protest (hoist a protest flag at once); normally this entails paying a protest fee which is forfeited should the protest fail. Most clubs have specific rules about this.

(h) Before each race the commodore or the racing committee of a club will issue duplicated or printed instructions. Do study these if you enter for the race. Study them before the race. Be sure you know the specified sound and flag signals.

(i) The details about the agreed course will specify which side the markers are to be passed on. If you *touch* a mark (even starting or finishing) you must retire from the race, unless it be proved that you were fouled and forced to touch it by another boat.

(j) Usually there are three sound signals (starting gun). The first time is a warning, saying that the race starts in 10 minutes. The second is the preparatory signal, meaning that it stars in 5 minutes and from that moment on you are under starter's rules, and a mistake could cost you the race, so watch it! Be afloat by the second signal.

(k) In difficult weather conditions several boats may make a false start. This will bring about a signal for all to return and await a fresh start. A collision would lead to both parties being disqualified.

(l) Start and Finish are judged as when *any one part* of a boat's hull crosses the appropriate line.

(m) If there is danger to life you must stop and assist another boat's crew. Hail them and ask if they need help. Failure to render assistance would lead to disqualification. Remember the job is to save the crew, the boat can probably be salvaged later. Nor are you allowed to desert your own crew if they fall overboard (or were they pushed?). So don't yield to the temptation if your mother-in-law makes a mistake while crewing for you; you have to stop and pick her up or lose the race.

(n) If you are unlucky enough to have an unfavourable position at the start of a race just grin and bear it; apply your technique to use the breeze to take you ahead. Check up with your club rules about the rights-of-way, especially when one boat might take the wind out of your sails.

Sailing is a difficult sport to organise for racing. The rules may seem difficult and severe but logic and necessity make them necessary so that the sport may exist. Do try to co-operate; obey the rules.

TIPS

Seek a clean wind (one whose current is not being absorbed by other sail).

Aim for midstream when there is a tide in your favour, avoid midstream if the tide is not with you.

Keep calm and keep the rules in spite of bad weather, tides, veering winds and the language used by your crew. Racing being what it is the first boat to cross the finishing line may still not be the winner.

A collection of cups is no substitute for good companionship, so do not let it become less than a sport.

Artificial sails shed water and don't absorb it; they are best for racing.

Keep slime and muck off the bottom (use scuba, and go down to scrub her).

heck the stores list.

A job worth doing is worth doing well.

Away with the breeze.

In an emergency—know your rope

Don't blame the wind; the sails react to your handling of them!

Always start your racing in a small boat, you'll learn more.

Three Points of Sailing

We have to start somewhere, so I think we will begin with *Running* which is the easiest to understand, but *not* the easiest to handle. The wind is behind you, coming over the stern (transom, most likely). No, generally speaking, in life you get nothing for free, and this is especially true of the wind at sea because for every advantage there is always a disadvantage or two. When the wind is behind you *all trimming of the sails is slower to take effect*.

1. Take care that the helmsman and the crew do not overbalance the boat (especially if she is small) because she will be more difficult to handle while running than at any other point of sailing: Experienced sailors notice it less than beginners.
2. It is essential to *watch the burgee* carefully and to judge the angle of the boat to the wind. Remember that a burgee is what a burgee does, and a ribbon or bit of rag on the forestay is just as good as an expensive club pennant.
3. Aim to get the billowing line of your mainsail at 90° in relationship to the fore-and-aft line of your boat. Remember I said *sail*, not the boom. If the boom were out at that angle the sail would tend to droop, and thus you would lose half of the power the wind offers you.
4. When running, aim to get your boom on the quarter facing that quarter from which the wind comes.
5. There is a position known as running free, which is with sails placed in *goosewing* position; it is very fast. The jibsail is held by a special jib-boom or jib stick. The mainsheet is usually carefully held by a stop-knot to control the extent to which it allows the mainsail to travel out. You would raise the centreboard in this position to speed up, and lower it to slow down. Never try running free when there is a hint of approaching bad weather, nor with a clumsy, inexperienced crew. The spinnaker is also used to achieve this (see below).

6. If you are using a *spinna[ker]* (... for beginners) remove the ... to the left, tell crew and ... the boom swings to the ... to extend until stopped. ... gybe is the centre (fore a[nd] ...
7. It is easier to misjudge ... when you are running th[e] ... ing. This means there is ... fortuitous gybe if the boa[t] ... Theoretically one could ... accidental gybe; in fact a ... don't take chances.
8. There is a risk of *pooping* while running. This means the waves can break over the stern, making the cockpit wet and uncomfortable, and often the cabin as well: In theory more often than in fact the weight of the water taken on board should capsize you, so if you have a heavy swell following you watch out for the possibility, and note carefully how much is coming in, and whether your self-draining cockpit is coping adequately. It can become a case of *water, water everywhere, nor any drop to drink.*
9. There is also a risk of broaching stemming from an accidental gybe, this is swinging broadside on into the trough of a wave.
10. If broaching occurs more than twice (and a wet business it is too) you are advised to stop everything and take in one reef; you have too much sail up for your own good.
11. There is another hazard—rolling; this is avoided by keeping a stern, muscular grip (not flabby) hand on the tiller; the broader the beam, the more seriously the rolling affects the ship. If she rolls so far that the boom dips in the sea, for that short moment of time your rudder is virtually useless; broaching and capsize could easily take place.

BEGINNER'S GUIDE TO SAILING

OF SAILING

1. RUNNING

With the wind

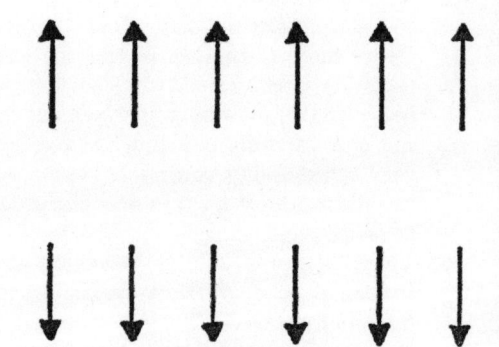

Against the wind

2 CLOSEHAULED

One sunny morning when the gulls were wheeling overhead, and the crisp salt wind was drying to the moisture of overnight on her rusting decks.

Bartimeus.

CLOSE HAULED

This is sailing against the wind. Some boats are more close winded than others, but no boat under sail can go 100% against the wind. Practically any boat can get about 45° to the wind, and the generally accepted procedure is to tack 45° to one side, and 45° to the other side. The idea is to tack as close to the wind as possible without letting the sails flap in idleness. The exact moment when you should tack comes only from experience and instinct; no book can teach you that, but if you are doing it in a wide river or estuary the rapid approach to the shore will be guide enough to start with. Try short tacks on a very fine day.

The length of any individual tack is affected by weather conditions. In very rough conditions it may be advantageous to make long tacks. The general theory is to keep the boom pointed towards the (port or starboard) transom, and work from there. Beginners try to sail far too close to the wind so they slow down too much. It is usually better to allow your craft to fall off of the wind a few degrees; take a longer tack but move faster overall.

When you see other boats which are near you and also sailing to windward it is easy to reach the conclusion that they are sailing more closely hauled than you are, that they are in fact faster. This is nearly always an optical illusion, and if you try to haul in to get a fraction more close hauled you will end up by going slower. I might go so far as to say that the beginner can hardly ever get faster by reducing the angle below 45°. With small waves one might succeed with a narrower angle. When you are sailing close hauled on the sea, *the solitude of centuries untold,* as W. C. Bryant says, you must pay careful attention to the tiller. This is because the direction of the wind is seldom pure, it changes direction, it changes speed with little or no warning.

The larger the waves the better it is to fall off a bit, ease the sheets out, this will keep your speed more constant.

If the boat is taken 100% into the wind she will be driven sternwards and the sails remain flapping uselessly; this is to be *in irons* if she won't pay off on a tack one way or the other or *in stays* if she is sulky but will eventually pay off.

If you are sailing as close hauled as possible with every

sail full of wind this is known as sailing *full and bye*.

An experienced yachtsman will be able to get incredibly narrow angles full and bye, but often this is with a racing boat whose keel or centreboard has been designed for this kind of work.

The work of the man at the tiller is every bit as important in utilising the wind as is the judging of the moment when one should tack.

The tiller is used to make up for sudden gusts of wind, pointing her into the direction of the wind (luffing up).

REACHING

This is the point of sailing which offers you most speed, and the sheer thrill of gliding effortlessly through the water leaving a foaming white wake behind you.

(If you are racing there is one thought I would add. In the *Alias Smith and Jones* TV series Ben Murphy once remarked: *Grudges are for people with bad stomachs.** I like that; keep it a sport; never hold a grudge. See Footnote).

1. In reaching, the jib should keep more or less the same angle of billowing out as does the mainsail.
2. Do not keep your sheets too tight while reaching; it will cause your boat to make unnecessary leeway, and, what is worse, you will be losing wind.
3. The trim of the boat is very important in reaching; never let her go with the leeside rail touching the water; however fast and furious this may look to landlubbers ashore it means you will lose speed because of water *drag* (frictional) and loss of wind.
4. If you sail on a close reach it is usual to keep the crew to the windward side, and on a broad reach sit a little more to the stern.
5. Remember to watch the burgee; if the luff of the main-

---

* This is not only amusingly expressed but also medically correct, what is more, long held grudges may cause bad stomachs. See my *Concise Herbal Encyclopedia*.

REACHING

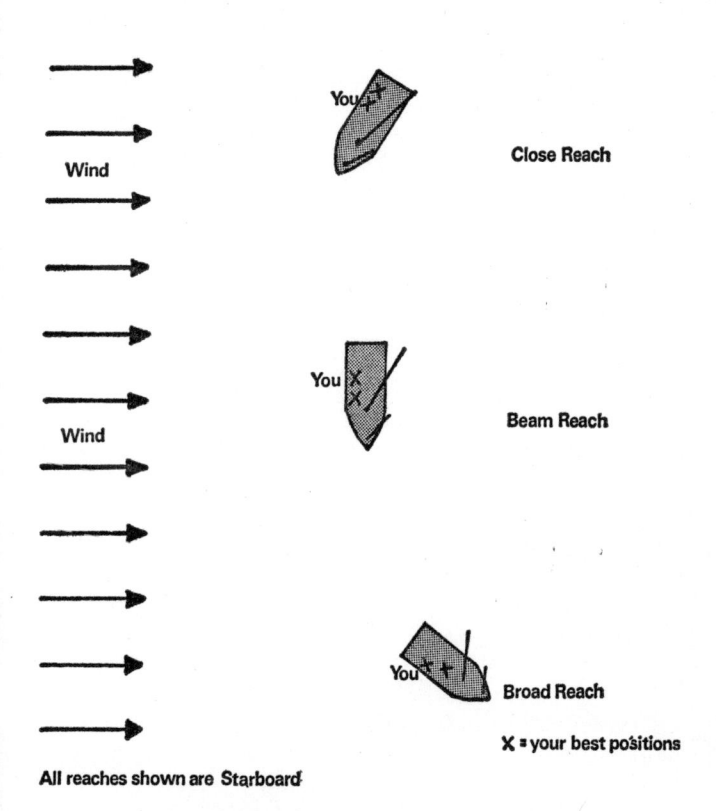

Close Reach

Beam Reach

Broad Reach

X = your best positions

All reaches shown are Starboard

sail shivers, just tighten the sheets slowly until the flapping stops.
6. In reaching, generally speaking, the wind is anticipated at 90° to the *sail*, and in dinghies the use of the kicking strap is common to keep her steady.

7. Do not hurry to shoot home; this may mean the sail is not used to its fullest potential, and it may pull your craft back on to a tack that you are trying to leave; only leisurely and firm handling are needed.
8. Boats have none of the suicidal tendencies of cars, and if in difficulties will usually swing round to a standstill, when the owner may collect his thoughts. Don't force your boat to wreck herself; if you are in a twist because of something going wrong let her swing to a halt while you find out where you missed out.

TACKING OR GOING ABOUT

Tacking—Turn the tiller! This enables you to get your boat to windward by sailing close-hauled with wind first starboard, then port side. The mainsail is kept fairly flat, and you make a zig-zag course to your point of destination. It requires bringing the bow across the wind, and is the opposite of gybing (q.v.).

In tacking, the helm is pushed away from the helmsman (put the helm down). Tacking must be done slowly and efficiently. As you change sides face the stern, never sideways; this way you can make sure that your boat is making the correct right angle when you tack; you will see it by the wake of the boat. Excessive thrust on the tiller can stop her dead. You must be sure that you are on the correct tack before you tighten the sheet. In tacking, the wind is in front of you and slows you down. A centreboard yacht may have to be turned more quickly than a keel boat because it is more likely to lose way during tacking. Tacking is slower than gybing.

If you are alone you may have to hold the tiller and the sheet in the same hand, otherwise avoid it. Change hands if you are solo, so that the *hand nearest the tiller is always holding that*. Experienced sailors tend to watch the wavelets to tell them the true direction of the wind rather than the burgee, especially during tacking.

As you turn the tiller, the bow crosses the eye of the wind, the sails flap dismally, you let go of the jibsheet you were holding, move across to the other side, facing the stern, seat yourself, pick up the other jibsheet, pull it through, and then

CLOSE HAULED TACKS

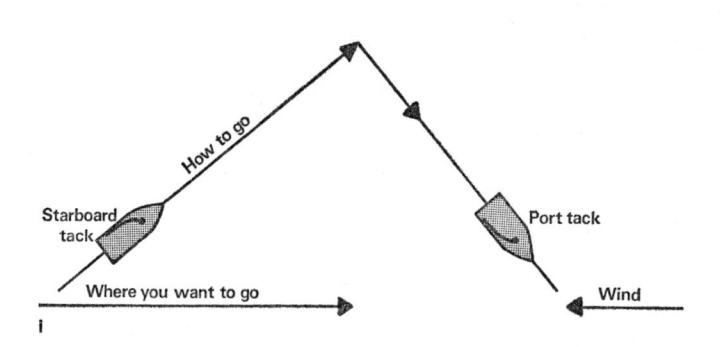

i

ii THE WAKE OF TACKING

you make a gentle adjustment to the mainsheet to haul it on to the new side. Slow and easy does it! If there is another member of the crew the mainsheet can be adjusted by one of you, whoever is not at the tiller.

GYBING
This is a much faster movement than tacking. Beginners often get a phobia about a gybe. Provided it is controlled there is nothing to fear, an accidental gybe is something else. With gybes the wind is astern, coming at you from behind; this

C*

means that the action of the wind on the mainsail is much stronger and faster. You (and any crew) get to the centre fore-and-aft line of the boat. If there is a strong wind you would move more aft and centre. If the tiller resists you it is necessary to exert more force. You must not let the boat heel because of the movement of the boom, or slide round into the wind.

The theory behind the gybe is that when the wind begins to blow on the same side as the mainsail you must change the boom and its sail to the leeward. The main difficulty is the fierceness with which wind will greedily try to snatch the sheet and its sail out of your hands. Remember to let the mainsheet run through your fingers fully; trying to restrain it while it is running may cause disaster, usually capsize; firstly let it run out fully, then slowly adjust as required. The tiller is pulled towards the helmsman (put the helm up).

Gybes must be made calmly, decisively and positively. When you see that the boom is twitching, *raring to go*, hesitate not, get it over, provided that nobody is forward, which could disturb the balance and perhaps let the rudder rise from its submerged position.

After every gybe check the steering carefully. Do shout out *gybe*! so that the crew can hear it.

A bad gybe in stormy weather may lead to dismasting, if not capsize. Do learn to gybe well, practise it regularly. Only the man who is unpractised is at risk.

Centreboard craft are most likely to capsize, keelboats to dismast.

Do not be satisfied in sailing or anything with being *just average*; do remember that to be just average is to be as near failure as success.

LUFFING

The *luff* is the edge of a sail that leads into the wind and weather. To luff is to swing your boat closer into the wind. (The edge of the sail farthest back from the wind is the leach.) The unusual word *luff* is found in Layamon's Brut (1205 A.D.) and relates back to the early Gothic *Lofa*, meaning the palm of the hand, to which the large paddle was once compared; in early ships this paddle was used to help the ship's helm keep on course, and its use began to be merged with the meaning it now has.

The luff of a foresail frequently has a bolt rope or wire stitched into it; this is useful for a beginner because it helps him to recognise which side of the sail it is.

Some close-hauled vessels will sail nicely straight if the helmsman lets her go for a while. This indicates good balance (and is something one *should* get in the price of the more expensive boat), but when the bows gentle towards the wind this is called *luffing up*, and the boat is then said to have *weather helm*. One which has *lee helm* is a boat that bears away from the wind. If you want to increase her weather helm you can stow ballast (that includes crew members for purposes of weight) further for'ard; either go for a smaller area of foresail (jib or what have you), put the foresail further back or enlarge the area of mainsail. As a long term, more permanent, measure you could have the mainmast raked further back. On a centreboard boat you would endeavour to get the board and rudder as deeply submerged as possible. For a lee helm, you would do the reverse of the measures given above.

As a general rule, the larger the area of jib the greater the pressure of wind for'ard of the mainmast; this induces the vessel to bear away; if the sail area fore and aft of the mast provides equal pressure the boat will not change direction noticeably; conversely, if the area of mainsail is larger and more effective, while the jib (or other foresail) is allowed to become useless (because of reduction of size or just flapping about) this makes the boat *luff up*. Understanding this, and practising it, makes for very expert tacking.

Luffing slows a vessel down, and should be done quickly enough to avoid stopping her dead, so trim your sheets before you lose steerage.

A word about *sheets*: these are ropes which govern the corners of a sail. The Old English *scýte* or *scéta*, meant a wide expanse of cloth such as one has as a sail or on a bed, and *sceát* meant a corner of the cloth, and a rope attached to the corner of the cloth was called a *sheet* (which *sh* is how the Anglo Saxons pronounced *sc*).

The more weather helm you get the harder it is for the helmsman of a small boat, and the rudder will begin to act as a brake; this is often due to badly-made sails, worn and stretched, or badly repaired, sails.

WHOA THERE!

Slowing down and stopping are as important for the beginner to learn as starting, if not more so.

Obviously, the first thing is to reduce partly or wholly the sail power, as is explained under the entry *Returning to Moorings*. But when the wind is sufficiently boisterous your vessel may be propelled along by the force of the wind against mast, doghouse, or crew standing on deck, so this is not a wholly infallible method. You can turn her to the wind so that she comes in irons, making no headway at all. This is often one of the quickest methods of stopping a ship, particularly if you are close-hauled at the time.

You can also *heave to* (past tense of the verb is *hove to*), which slows you down, virtually to a stop, and is useful if you want to pick up a passenger who went for a swim (voluntarily or otherwise), a floating case of currency notes, cask of rum, a lost dinghy or just a . . . mooring rope, (how prosaic can one get?). You start with the jib or foresail, let out the lee foresail sheet, haul in on the windward foresail sheet (some call *windward* the weather side, since wind is weather, and haul away until windward foresail sheet clew (corner) is right round and well to the weatherside of the mast. This is quickly done, and is a very seamanlike manoeuvre, because it means that the foresail forces the bows of your vessel to leeward, which negatives the direction forwards that comes from the aerofoil action of the mainsail. You either hold the tiller for as long as you wish, or lash it to leeward if you want to make a period stop in that position (such as if your friend is going down with scuba equipment to look for sunken treasure galleons).

When hove to you will probably make some leeway drift but to all intents and purposes not much headway.

MAN OVERBOARD

Worse things happen at sea, bibulous mariners used to assure landlubbers when I was young. Indeed, any casualty at sea seems more difficult because the wretched water and wind keep moving. Your best friend (the one who owes you a couple of hundred) has just been swept overboard, you must save his life! How to do it? Your first noble instinct will be to throw a lifebelt so that he has some token to remember you by while you turn about to come back and get him. This sentiment is indeed marred if your lifebelt is thrown at the candidate for a long swim, who may then be crowned rather than drowned. However capable of floating, the lifebelts weigh heavy enough. Throw this support *towards* the victim. He will see it coming and swim towards it (don't take anybody (or anything) to sea who cannot swim—or on a boat round a shallow lake either for that matter).

You simply tack or gybe and turn until you can come alongside your friend, heave to if need be, and haul him aboard. If possible one person should keep an eye on his exact position, because even with safety orange or yellow clothing a small head in an ocean full of waves can be difficult enough to find.

CAPSIZE, AND HOW TO COME OUT OF IT LAUGHING

Wind and waves have bad manners; they rarely announce their erratic wills to the beginner (experienced sailing folk are canny and can deduce changes from weather conditions the beginner is scarcely aware of). The speed with which wind can change is scarcely credible to one who is not accustomed to it, and an unwished for gybe may end in capsize, so that your boat dips its sails into the water which soaks into them, making them heavy and virtually useless, the rudder is out of the water and no longer helps you at all.

A capsize is a nuisance and a wetting, it should never be anything more. In racing one sees boats capsized, righted, and finish up by taking a prize after they regain their speed, so what's the worry?

A light boat is more likely to capsize than others. But keep to the rules! Never abandon your boat. She is bigger and easier to spot than a sadly bobbing head of some lone swimmer.

Never remove your *clumsy* lifejacket to swim ashore; *Davy Jones's Locker* is full to overflowing with drowned people who did just that. It isn't swimming: it is the coldness and pro-

CAPSIZE
1 HOW IT HAPPENS

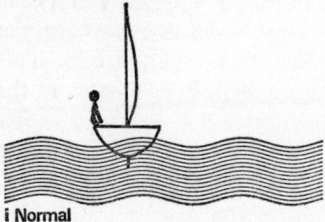

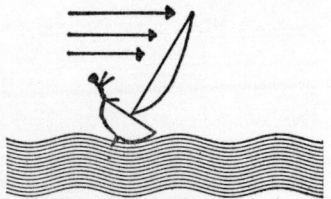

i Normal

ii a. Sudden heavy gust of wind
b. Rudder out of water
c. Sails go down to the water

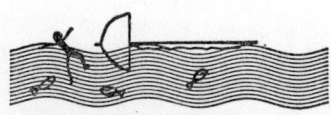

iii Visiting the fish at home

2 WHAT TO DO

i Stand on windward side of centreboard

ii Climb on board

iii Reef your sails quickly to avoid the likelihood of another capsize

longed exposure to it (which can numb you) that is the real danger.

'Never take a river or lake type open boat out to sea' is a general rule. Some exceptionally gifted, brave and talented people have sailed (even rowed) open boats across the Atlantic etc. Until you think you have their ability don't risk it. Many of the so-called yachting disasters that the press headlines come about because people take a boat they can barely handle on a millpond into conditions for which the vessel was never designed. Lifejackets should be worn whenever conditions require it.

A solo yachtsman should wear a lifeline attached to standing rigging. Hold lines attached to standing rigging are advisable if you are at sea and the conditions turn nasty. Then you can move across the deck, clutching support however she rolls, pitches, etc.

A large bailer (plastic bucket) should be firmly attached by string and ready for use. A smaller bailer for final mopping up is also required. Never go to sea or into an estuary if you cannot swim (Consult my book *Beginner's Guide to Swimming and Water Sports*).

Never just let bad conditions develop without taking avoiding action—See the section on *Storms*—and make haste to reef one or two. Better slow down and arrive safely!

A wooden boat with no ballast is virtually unsinkable: although she may sink to a distressingly low position in the water she will keep afloat and keep up. A glassfibre or resin-based boat invariably has built-in buoyancy, and occasionally additional watertight compartments which make her unsinkable. The greatest danger lies in a boat with shifting ballast (chains in the bilge, etc.), and these are now mostly historic, rarely being encountered. A good deep keel, however heavy, guards you against capsize. If you have artificial buoyancy to help you, keep it high up in the hull, never low down—which would deteriorate her stability factor. Dinghies and craft without keels proper are the most likely to capsize for with a real keel capsize is virtually impossible in a well-designed boat. The general rule is to get amidships on the windward side, stand on the centre board, grasp the gunwale and haul away until she rights herself.

The quicker the righting after capsize the easier it will be and as soon as she is upright get those sails lowered. The last thing you need is a second capsize. The coldness of the water may be too much a strain for the efficiency of your muscles, but unless you get her upright and stabilise her position you could be in and out of the water like a yo-yo. Such crew of yours as went overboard with you should climb over the transom. Don't forget to tell them they did well (I'm sure they did). Now have a look at the boat. Most probably more water is coming in through the housing of the centreboard. One of you can plug the housing with anything that will slow down the entry of more water (good use for the scarf your mother-in-law gave you last Christmas: the one that doesn't match anything at all); all others present must bail. If it is any consolation to you at this moment in time Kenichi Horie spent practically a whole night and day bailing out during a typhoon (just thought it would cheer you up). When you have got the water out, the boat floating at her normal waterline, you proceed on your way. If a vacuum flask of hot cocoa survived the upset, now is the time to pass it round.

In very light racing craft an experienced sailing crew can right the boat in a few minutes without lowering sails. In severe weather you usually have to release the halyards from their cleats, bunch the sail down to the boom before standing on the centreboard; this makes certain the sail is down before she is righted.

One of the advantages of having ropes, fenders and the like on the boat is that during capsize they are handy to hang on to while you get your breath and stand by for your righting effort.

Do practise a deliberate capsize once or twice a season on a really warm calm day with a friend standing by in his boat.

If you see someone capsize, especially in racing conditions do call out and ask if they want help before barging in and giving it, unasked. If they are racing they could lose the race by accepting help!

WARNING
1. Never try to right a boat from the leeward; she may roll over on top of you.
2. You should never be without your lifejacket if there is the slightest possibility of capsize. Don't promise to fit it on while in the water, that is too late.

Theory of Sailing

This is the aspect of the subject which some authors explain in considerable detail, which is helpful if you are an expert in maths, and confusing sometimes if you aren't.

The following simplification may not satisfy all readers, but I hope it will serve to introduce the important details.

There are three things to study in sailing—the wind, the water, and the boat.

Until recent times there were few craft in the world which were as perfectly designed as the earliest craft that sailed the ancient Nile in the time of King Akhnaten, and the wooden long ships of the Vikings (often constructed without a single nail, using wooden dowels instead).

The shape, length, beam, draught (depth) of a boat, the height of the mast, and the shape of sails all affect the performance of a boat. (The depth and size of keel being basically part of the overall draught.)

The truth of the matter is that whatever design you have it is limited to one purpose more than others, so what will help you when running may be a positive drawback when going close-hauled, and so on.

A good sailor is fundamentally a man who knows his boat, knows her every change of behaviour in every possible situation, and knows how to handle her to his own best advantage.

One of the difficulties connected with enthusiastic amateur boat conversions is that they often neglect to consider what the end result will be on a boat's performance.

The progress of the boat is affected by the slot effect of wind on the sails, the different speed of wind passing a sail to leeward working against that passing the sail to windward forcing the sail to influence the boat.

This is modified (helped or hindered) by the balance of wind pressure and the lateral resistance given by the water.

Further complicated explanations are necessary when you have wind with tide, and wind against tide, but these are rather for the more advanced sailor who is far beyond the practical necessities of the beginner.

THE BEGINNER'S GUIDE TO SAILING 83

THEORY OF SAILING

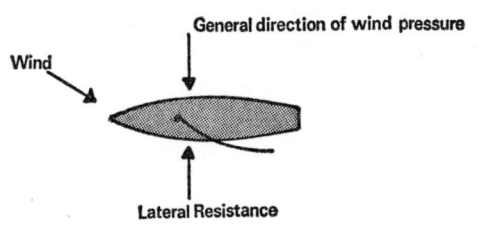

Wind
General direction of wind pressure
Lateral Resistance

i THE IMPACT OF LATERAL RESISTANCE

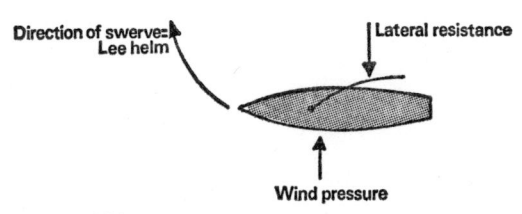

Direction of swerve= Lee helm
Lateral resistance
Wind pressure

ii VARIATION 1

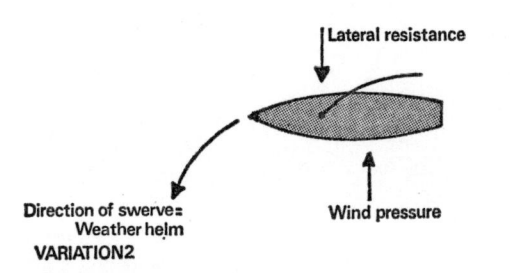

Lateral resistance
Direction of swerve= Weather helm
Wind pressure

VARIATION 2

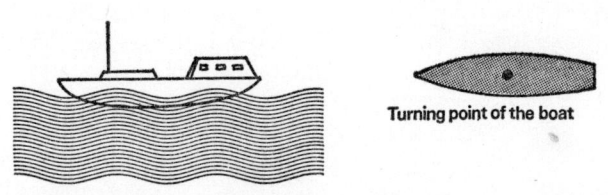

Turning point of the boat

iii ALTERATIONS TO STRUCTURE CHANGE WEIGHT DISPOSITION AND THUS THE TURNING POINT

THE WAYS OF THE WIND

Matthew Arnold spoke of the *sand-strewn caverns cool and deep: where the winds are all asleep,* but except for a spell in the doldrums the sailor is unlikely to experience the slumbers of the winds, rather the opposite, even the sort of storms concerning which Andrea Karkavitsas declared *Cain, after his crime, should have been sentenced to a sailor's life.*

Wind conditions vary from hour to hour, day to day and month to month: No book can detail exactly what sort of conditions you may meet beyond the coast, estuaries and rivers where men start to sail, but I can give some generalisations that will help beginners.

1. A wind blowing past you on to the shore will always seem to produce rougher conditions than really exist.
2. Conversely, a wind blowing towards you from off the shore is producing weather that is rougher than it looks.
3. Winds rise with a flood tide and die with an ebb tide most of the time around coast and harbours.
4. If you are offshore and getting very windswept and sea-wet, slow her down, and take her home as vertically as you can.
5. If in a small boat do not become a fugitive from foam and spray. A sudden, ill-judged move to dodge dampness could overbalance and capsize the craft. The worse the wind, the slower the crew should move in a small boat.
6. When the rain comes first the wind that follows it will be much rougher than when wind comes first.
7. The old sea-dog keeps an eye open for a long dark line on the water, caused by wind ruffling the waves up, and gets ready to ease his sheet; this does not mean that the real squall will hit you from that direction whence came the darkening line. The old hand never panics, he just uses that boisterous blow to get home safe and dry.

> *Stands the Church clock at ten to three?*
> *And is there honey still for tea?*
> As Rupert Brooke said of home.

8. Nothing to do with winds really, but *never* set sail on a Friday! Two minutes before midnight on Thursday, two

minutes after midnight on Friday, then it is Saturday! But never on a Friday, if you want to get back alive, that is.

9. Winds change direction unexpectedly; don't forget to change your position (calmly) if you are in a small boat that needs counterbalance.
10. If you are in coastal or estuarine waters and the wind begins to play havoc with you, a beginner, at a time when you are in doubt what you should do then *drop* sail, calmly row your dinghy (or small boat) ashore. There is never any shame in getting your boat, your crew (if any) and yourself back safely. If some loud-mouthed know-it-all begins to make fun of this, say in a loud, clear voice, that you did it because you doubted whether he was a good enough sailor to rescue you if you had capsized—he who laughs last laughs best! Often the loudmouths are those who go out and don't get back— ever.
11. Wind is cold. Spray is wet; when you are wet your body loses heat in trying to evaporate the wet on your skin, and you get colder. So if you see a wind coming out of what Tennyson's Tithonus called

    The ever silent spaces of the East,
    Far-folded mists and gleaming of morn,

    Make haste to get that other pullover on, and don your oilies (though these are seldom made of oiled cloth nowadays, rather of plastic, nylon, etc).
12. If you want to use a powerful wind to get you in you would lift the centreboard only if you could estimate fairly accurately that the leeward drift wouldn't pile you up on the rocks.
13. When the wind begins to rage, if you are crewing, do be man enough to take the captain's orders, even if he is your elder brother, cousin, friend, husband etc. As Mark Twain said in his immortal *Innocents Abroad*: If five cooks can spoil the broth, what may not five captains do with a pleasure excursion?
14. Wind and tide in the same direction give a smooth surface to the sea. Against each other the surface without doubt will get very rough.

15. It's an ill wind that blows nobody good. Do not get wild with the wind; it is only doing its job! Somebody, somewhere, is benefiting from it even if momentarily you aren't.

THE BEAUFORT SCALE

Many of us who sit at a tiller, in the words of Herman Melville's poem, *watching the lone bird's flight round the spar, where mid-sea surges pour,* should give a kindly thought to Admiral Sir Francis Beaufort (1774-1857) who in 1805 invented the scale named after him. It analyses wind velocity into 12 divisions, as listed below. In the minds of yachting men at a club meeting, the force of wind according to Beaufort is often multiplied by two when talking of a storm they encountered successfully, particularly if no other club member was there!

An annual prize was instituted at the Royal Naval College (for success in Navigation etc.) in honour of Admiral Beaufort. Here is the scale in simplified form:

Force no.	*Wind*	*Speed in knots*	*Notes*
0	Calm	Below 1	... Sea glassy
1	Light air	1-3	Smoke ashore goes straight up. Ripples on water.
2	Light Breeze	4-6	Wind vanes ashore moved. Slight crests on waves.
3	Gentle Breeze	7-10	Flags blown out fully. Crests begin to break up.
4	Moderate Breeze	11-16	Small waves, white tops on many of them.
5	Fresh Breeze	17-21	Deeper, longer waves, most of them have white tops, Medium sized craft would tend to shorten sail.

Force no.	Wind	Speed in knots	Notes
6	Strong Breeze	22-27	Large waves, much spray. Quite loud whistling in rigging. Definitely double reefing.
7	Moderate Gale	28-33	Scudding foam, Longer, larger waves. Life on deck decidedly uncomfortable.
8	Fresh Gale	34-40	A lot of water getting into the wind. Foam flying, and if you've not made harbour—good luck!
9	Strong Gale	41-47	Waves getting uncomfortably tall, seemingly solid chunks of water fly about, landing heavily on deck.
10	Whole Gale	48-55	Cheer up, ashore trees are being rooted up and thrown about! Waves now very high, so much foam and spray you can barely see anything.
11	Storm	56-64	Any lone yachtsman who started out an atheist will be cured of that by now. This is the sort of thing for which Cape Horn is famed.
12	Hurricane	Above 64	Some brilliant sailors have survived one, not many.

A TIDE IN THE AFFAIRS OF MEN—AND WEATHER AS WELL

Sailing, said my friend's wife, *would be marvellous if only the weather didn't keep changing.* What we cannot alter we must endure, so let us see what we can learn about it.

The Golden Rule is: Clouds are blown along in front of the weather that blows them along. Watch the clouds; it is not easy to tell always what they mean, but practice and experience teach you quickly.

For those who live in the northern hemisphere there is another rule, do not trust a north-easter, for as the writer *Bartimeus* used to say, it is treacherous.

One useful, if not essential, gadget is a barometer, but don't bother unless you learn how to read it in conjunction with weather signs. Continuous readings are essential if you are at sea or in coastal waters. In the temperate zones a reading every 5-6 hours is advised. Particularly use it in connection with radio weather forecasts. Now to start, some simplified interpretations:

1. Barometer falling at the time when the wind changes direction means that a Force 7, 8 or higher wind is on its way.
2. Barometer rising but wind force rising rapidly means you should expect a severe squall; batten down the hatches, take in a reef.
3. Barometer falling with heavy clouds forming on the horizon; Force 6 or above coming, expect trouble.
4. Barometer rising, air drying out—Strong wind coming soon.
5. Rising slowly, south wind strengthening indicates settled fair weather.
6. Rising quickly, wind veering SW to NW means fair weather now, maybe rain tomorrow.
7. Rising from a low reading, west wind strengthening, clearing up but getting colder.
8. Rising, wind veering S-SW good weather for some days ahead.
9. Steady reading, air drying out. Fair weather for some days.
10. The faster the fall of a barometer the more quickly will weather worsen.
11. Fast fall, reading less than 30, expect at least Force 8 and rotten weather.

12. Fast fall, below 30, E or NE wind. (Or E-N.) Rain or snow on the way. *Beware of ice* forming on deck and rigging; this must be chipped off quickly, particularly in the far north; its weight could sink you.
13. Slow fall, E to NE wind. Light showers and slight swell.
14. Rapid fall S-SE wind. Rain coming, about 12 hours away.
15. Slow fall S-SE wind. Rain coming, about 24 hours away.
16. Slow fall SE-NE veering. Rain about 12 hours off. Rough weather coming.
17. The faster the fall of barometer readings the more easily recognisable are the changes in cloud formations.
18. Fairly fast fall and mares' tails clouds mean rain, strong wind and a depression are coming at you.

The origin of the word *gale* could come from the Old English word *galan*—to sing (as in nightingale) or from the old Norse *gal*—crazy. Either is an adequate description of the wind's behaviour.

If bad weather strikes you and your boat make some allowance for any crew you have aboard; they may suffer from what Mark Twain (*The Innocents Abroad*) called the *Oh my* feeling: *He put his hand on his stomach and said oh my, and reeled away*. The more storms you have weathered together the less likely are the crew to experience sickness, which is as often psychological, and largely due to the cold and the wet. If you are used to bad weather don't be intolerant of those with less experience.

CLUES IN THE CLOUDS

There are many specialised books that will teach you by photographs what the variations in clouds mean. Clearly these are specifically related to certain geographic areas (which this work is not), but for the beginner the following general diagrams will help in interpreting the clues in the clouds.

Remember—to predict the weather accurately is to have time to think how best to use it to your advantage; do learn as much about the weather as possible.

In the words of the Simon and Garfunkel song, sailing can be *a bridge over troubled waters*: use good seamanship to get across.

A cloud is composed of a mass of small particles of water condensed by the air cooling into a vapour; the height at which the clouds exist distinguishes them from fog or mist. The general classification is High, Middle, Lower and Vertical (such as some Cumulo Nimbus, thunder clouds, etc.). Cirrostratus and Cirrus exist about 30,000 ft. They are wispy and thin. Cirrocumulus are ball-like tufts of clouds, Altostratus seem like thick, twisted strands of old rope which begin about 16,000 ft. but may ascend to 24,000 ft. Altocumulous (the poet's *mackerel sky*) are larger fish-like tufts around 13,000 ft. Nimbostratus are almost vertical clouds of rain whose lower part starts around 6,500 ft. and whose heads can reach double that height. A bulbous cumulonimbus cloud can have its base as low as 5,000 ft. and its egg-like dome thundering four times that height; it is the result of ascending currents of air. It is invariably accompanied by thunder and heavy rain, and is a curse to airmen as well as seamen.

Lower clouds prevent the loss of too much heat by the Earth's or ocean's surface and protect them from the strength of the sun's rays.

TIME AND TIDE WAIT FOR NO MAN

This is one of the earliest proverbs I learnt as a child; it is found in many languages, and is solidly true. *This sea, whose gently, awful stirrings seem to speak of some hidden soul beneath,* wrote Herman Melville, and the tides are the most obvious signs of the stirrings. Tides are vertical in effect. Tidal streams are horizontal. The movements of the two vary in every locality, usually according to season of the year etc. For unknown waters they are usually to be found in a nautical almanac or local publication. The tidal stream particularly affects a sailing boat's performance as she seeks to come in alongside a jetty or take up a mooring.

In reading tide tables you must know the meaning of the following:

MHWS — Mean high water, Springs
MHWN — Mean high water, Neaps
MLWS — Mean low water, Springs
MLWN — Mean low water, Neaps

APPROXIMATE HEIGHT & CLOUD CLASSIFICATION

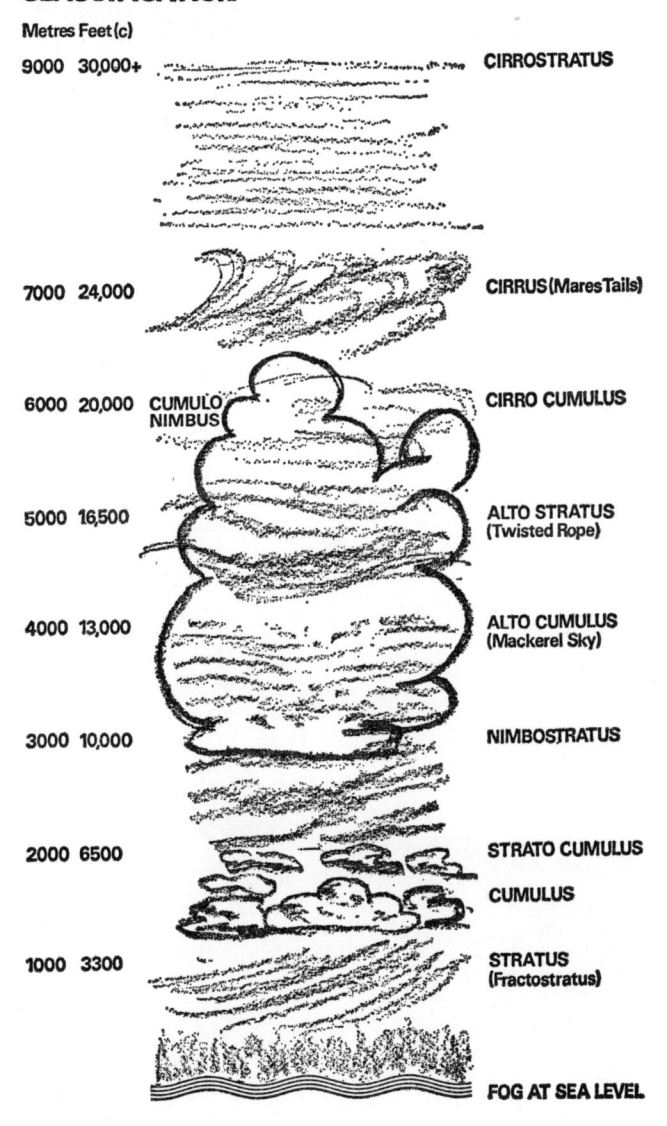

Metres Feet (c)

9000	30,000+	**CIRROSTRATUS**
7000	24,000	**CIRRUS (Mares Tails)**
6000	20,000	CUMULO NIMBUS / **CIRRO CUMULUS**
5000	16,500	**ALTO STRATUS** (Twisted Rope)
4000	13,000	**ALTO CUMULUS** (Mackerel Sky)
3000	10,000	**NIMBOSTRATUS**
2000	6500	**STRATO CUMULUS** / **CUMULUS**
1000	3300	**STRATUS** (Fractostratus)
		FOG AT SEA LEVEL

CLOUDS

1 CIRRUS
Very high, like wisps of a horse's tail

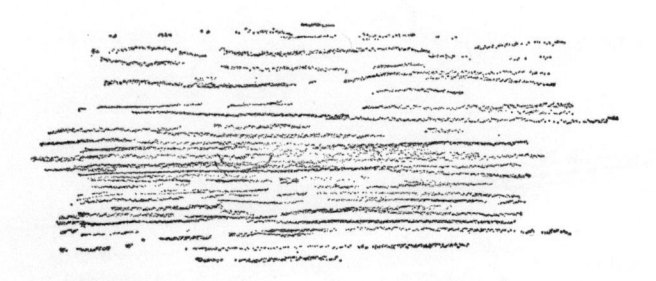

2 CIRROSTRATUS
Thin white strips or a sheet which can cloak the whole sky

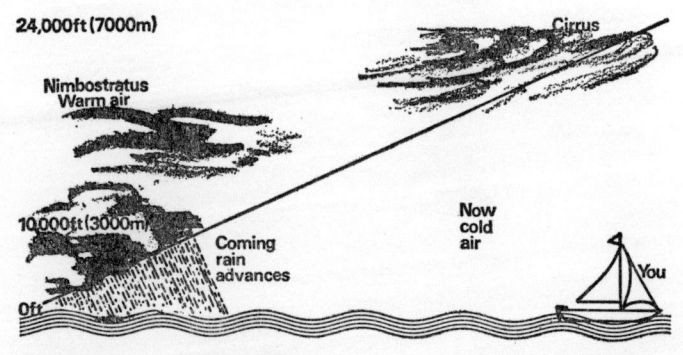

24,000ft (7000m) — Cirrus

Nimbostratus
Warm air

10,000ft (3000m)
Coming rain advances

Now cold air

You

0ft

3 A TYPICAL WEATHER PATTERN

CIRRUS 'FEATHERS' & THICKER CIRROSTRATUS

ALTOSTRATUS MAKING A WATERY LIGHT OF THE SUN

CUMULO NIMBUS FORMING

TIDES

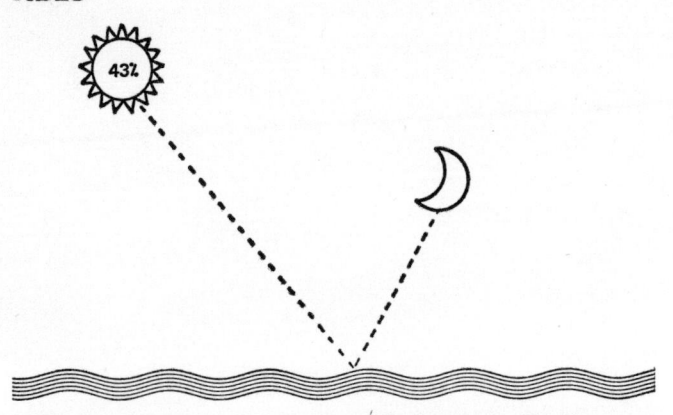

The sun, farther off than the moon, exerts only 43% of the moon's pull on tides

One of the first things a beginner has to learn is that a Spring Tide is not related to a season of the year; it comes about 36 hours after New Moon and Full Moon. Neap Tides come about seven days after each Spring Tide; they are the slowest tides and the Spring Tides and Tidal Streams are the fastest. These rise very high and sink very low on ebb (due to the earth being in a straight line with the sun and the moon both of which then exert forces on the tides). Tidal streams are usually measured in knots.

In open or estuarine (semi-open) waters the ebb is frequently faster than the wind, and occasionally one may see (to the hilarious enjoyment of all those ashore) a ship being swept backwards; it is, of course, less fun for those on board who are struggling to control her.

In some places there are freak tide conditions. One place in Japan has a high and a low simultaneously within a couple of miles of each other, but normally you can calculate a straight 6 hours flood and 6 hours ebb. You can try to plan your cruising so that you can use the tidal stream to help you instead of battling against it. It is often 7 flood, 5 ebb, etc. Check locally. Do use the printed data available to get the speed of a local tidal stream if you sail with the wind and the stream in your favour you will move along like lightning!

With the average-sized craft (up to 8 tons) 2-3 extra knots can be gained. Shallow water effects can cause two high tides to one low tide in some places. At the Spring and Autumn equinoxes exceptionally extreme high and low *Spring tides* occur; the danger is that a beginner might run aground during an ebb and have to wait for the next equinox to float him off again!

There are some places where a tidal stream sets up some turbulence as it meets a current or more forceful stream (i.e. round a headland, etc.). This is called a *race* and it is often a race to keep a small dinghy upright in it. If you are mooring in tidal waters do allow for extra chain or cable so that a rising flood won't yank you out of your anchorage, etc.

And, lastly, however good the tide, don't set sail on a Friday. It's not a superstition, just a fact; something always goes wrong if you begin a voyage on a Friday; a jaunt down river you'd get away with, but into the estuary, coastal waters or open sea—well, I wouldn't.

Navigation

This is a subject of which you can get only a smattering from any book; it is also something you can learn, like driving a car, very quickly with a little practice.

This section outlines the sort of thing you learn in studying navigation, and provides some of the essential facts with which you must be armed before you begin to add to your education.

For the purpose of making a chart the earth, which is somewhat pear-shaped, is shown as a sphere. It rotates towards the east, where the sun *rises*.

To measure the distances of sea and land imaginary lines of latitude have been adopted which are based on the equator. Then we speak of North or South Latitude to give a position. This method has been known in one form or another since the days of the Vikings. Less sure is the antiquity of Longitude lines, which are now (since the 17th century) based on the meridian at Greenwich: these lines meet in the Pacific, at the International Date Line (where yesterday becomes tomorrow) in the Pacific Ocean at 180° (it varies to include the Aleutian Isles with Alaska, and some of the South Pacific islands with Australia). Compared with sun time one complete hour is lost for every 15° of the globe passed when circumnavigating the world.

If you are a mariner you get used to reading directions for finding a harbour or place such as this:

$$56° \; 5' \; 10'' \; N \; \text{(Latitude)}$$
$$10° \; 25' \; 5'' \; E \; \text{(Longitude)}$$

We invariably quote latitude first. Measurements are expressed in degrees shown by ° after a figure. Each degree is divided into 60 minutes; each minute is shown by the sign ' written after a figure. Each minute contains 60 seconds which are written as '' after a figure. 90° make a right angle, as in ordinary mathematics.

This is not complicated but a wonderful way of measuring distance over a continually moving liquid, etc.

Then when we want to estimate how far a ship is from har-

All help is appreciated.

The call of the running tide.

Two means the work is halve

NAVIGATION

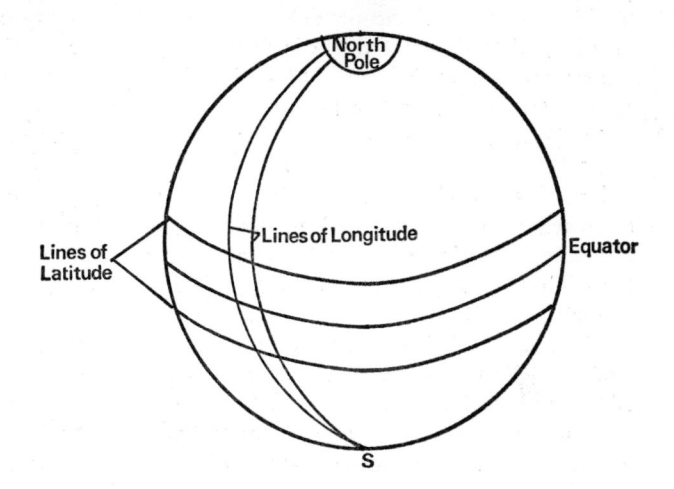

Diagram of a globe showing North Pole, South Pole (S), Lines of Latitude, Lines of Longitude, and Equator.

bour, etc. we speak of the Nautical Mile (one *minute*). In fact, because the earth has its peculiar shape this varies from 6,046 ft. at the equator to 6,108 at the polar regions (seamen work on an average of 6,080 ft.).

The mile is divided into tens, and one tenth is called a *Cable*.

For depth the Old English word *fæfom* is used, each fathom is 6 feet.

The word for a map of the sea is *chart*, and it is important to look for the *scale* on which the chart is constructed. Maybe it is 1/250,000, meaning one inch represents 250,000 inches of real earth (sea) surface, maybe 1/500,000 etc.

For safety's sake do check on the *date* of the chart; some harbours have silted up through neglect; there are shallows where 20 years back there were none; maybe for some commercial reason a shoal shown 10 years back has been dredged out of existence. These precautions are important for the beginner; an old hand will often steer beautifully with a chart that any museum would be proud to own.

A chart is covered with a maze of figures, diagrams etc.

D

Each chart will explain in footnotes what these mean; in time you get used to the fact that a certain type of print is being used to give you fathoms depth of water, while another typeface is used to show the depth in feet of the shallows.

Letters such as S—sand, M—mud, R—rocks, etc, are quickly learnt and most of them are instinctively understood after the first 30 minutes of looking seriously at your first chart.

Really good charts, especially those showing you the approaches to harbours and moorings, etc. will give the direction of tidal streams, and the speed at which they flow for High Tide, and Neap and Spring tides. Most coasts have one specific place from which all High Tides are measured. In England the High Water time is usually reckoned on Dover and related to so many hours after the exact time of New Moon and Full Moon.

In well-used sea lanes, approaches to harbours, etc. buoys are used. The system varies slightly in different countries, and it is important to get from a club, or yacht chandler, the coloured folder or brochure which is invariably available of the system in use on your own coastline. Usually the system in use follows this sort of pattern.

Buoys that you keep on the starboard side when entering the area are black, or checks of black and white, maybe with a sign or a flashing light on the top.

Buoys that you keep on the portside when entering the area are usually red or chequered red and white, with signs or flashing light on the top.

Green Buoys are used to mark a wreck or submerged ship.

Green and white horizontal stripes may indicate that you are entering a minefield or a naval target firing area—get out quick!

Yellow and black striped buoys are used to indicate sewage disposal areas, so do not fish near these—or swim!

Never get worried by books that list dozens of different kinds of buoy colours; remember that you are unlikely to meet a tenth of the colourful variations on any normal cruise or voyage.

As for learning about the compass, at last people have got round to using the simple numbers of the 360° compass, and it is unusual to be required to learn all the fancy bits about East Nor East by East stuff—unless you are sailing an old windjammer and want to be in character. Whereas the compass you got out of a Christmas cracker (with a jolly motto besides) would be better than none at all at sea, you would be wiser to discard the dry (needle on card) compass in favour of a fluid compass, which in larger yachts is fixed nicely in gimbals; this gives it the ability to stay upright, readable, and comparatively still whatever rolling, pitching etc. the boat is suffering.

A good ship's compass points to Magnetic North (70° 40′ N. 96° 30′ W) which cuts out one set of variations to be reckoned with; a dry compass shows True North.

A ship's compass is fitted with two parallel lines which give the exact fore and aft lines of your ship (provided it was properly fitted); if your course is set for 20°, or 50° you just keep the compass so that the lubber's lines are opposite the degrees of course chosen. This cannot be left, for howsoever you lash the helm (wheel) a boat will stray off course like an uninstructed human, and continual attention to the helm is needed to put her back on course again.

Variation of Magnetic North position is noted from year to year, and the precise position will be easterly or westerly according to which hemisphere you are in. *Most charts mark this in,* much is done to make life easy for yachtsmen now. Variation depends upon place.

A compass should be kept away from the galley and the anchor and cable lockers because it can suffer from *deviation* caused by any iron or steel aboard ship (a metal thermos flask even) that is brought near it. When a new boat is launched it is customary for the deviation to be worked out, and this must be recorded and deducted from every calculation made for position; very simple in practice. Deviation depends upon each individual boat.

You are sitting down at your yacht's chart table, your sextant, your parallel rules, dividers, pencils (and rubber eraser), logbook and the compass reading before you with the brand new chart and a sheet of transparent paper over it (so that you can use the chart many times). You draw a nice line from A to B, this represents where you want to go, and where your boat would go if she were a seagull (whatever her name). This is called the True line course.

If there is an easterly variation you subtract this to the True, or if westerly you add it to the True (e.g. True 90° var. 7° E: 83° Magnetic Course). But your delightful ship has a built-in deviation of 4°W, so that you now add this on to the previous figure, and we get a Compass Course of 87°. (Ten minutes practice in adding and subtracting is enough to last you a lifetime afloat, just remember *Easterly eats the number away, Westerly wins a number on.*)

After that you make allowances for tides, leeway caused by wind action (judge by the angle of the log trailed astern). If, for any reason you wanted to calculate backwards from Compass to True line you would then add instead of subtract, and vice-versa. A navigator must learn a great deal about tides, and (if seagoing or coastal) would be wise to have a nautical almanac on board showing expected high and low water figures when he approaches what Matthew Arnold refers to as *the lone line of spray where the sea meets the moon-bleach'd sand.*

The relevant authority in each country publishes a detailed chart of tidal streams, so that the wise mariner may set sail accordingly to catch a favourable stream (even so never set sail on a Friday, it's always unlucky—no, I'm not superstitious, it *is* just unlucky, ask any sailor).

Don't be deceived by the know-all who proudly asserts he never learnt any navigation at all; what would he do on one of those occasions when *with sloping masts and dipping prow* he finds his little craft trapped in a sea mist *through fog-smoke white glimmered the white moon-shine* (Coleridge), the awful white nothingness that many seagoing sailors experience, then you may find it too late to start learning navigation!

On coastal trips it is possible to take bearings from landmarks which are easily visible, but you must base this on cross-bearings; between 30° and 120° you will get the most reliable readings from two bearings.

With the advent of electronic equipment many of the early ingenious aids to navigation are falling into disuse, although they have, like the log line, the advantage that they can work without electricity.

The log line was marked in knots, enabling a seaman to learn easily at what speed his vessel is moving, and a similar line was thrown overboard to take soundings, with coloured ties attached to a rope at specified intervals of measurement. A leaden weight made sure it sank quickly to the bottom—unlike modern echo-sounders it never broke down, or if the line snapped could be replaced at virtually no cost.

Sailing club libraries are usually full of books which will prepare you for navigation, but try to learn most of it afloat with an experienced sailor. It is much more fun that way.

ELECTRONIC AIDS

If you are planning extensive offshore or deep water cruising you would be well advised to find what electronic aids are available. I am not in favour of gadgets because with the best servicing in the world they may occasionally break down, and modern man is often hopeless and helpless without them. My advice is: use an electronic aid only if you do know what to do (maybe with a textbook in your left hand) without them. To go to sea relying solely upon instruments, and to be unable to get back without them is a dangerous, alluring deception.

An electronic log can be obtained; and echo sounders are two a penny, so many are the designs and makes, most of them very good for the field of their operations.

An echo sounder is a useful refinement because it saves a lot of guess-work if you are in misty conditions off some barely-known coastline with shoals and mudbanks all around you.

Many of the small boat radar reflectors are regarded as ornamental cult symbols rather than practical, but the introduction of transponders at the masthead (they emit their own signal when set off by another boat's radar scan and prevent collision) does much to give the safety which radar was designed to provide. If buying radar devices ask *how* far they are effective and calculate how much time to manoeuvre out of difficulty that distance would give you at your usual knots average speed.

For long voyages VHF radio-telephones which are fully transistorised can keep contact with people ashore. Most of those who go on long solo voyages use these for up-to-date professional weather forecasts etc. Direction-finding loops, auto pilots, auto direction finders, wind speed indicators, water speed meters and various other apparatus is available to him who can pay for it.

Although not truly electronic, one small useful refinement is a tide watch invented by a Swiss firm. When you set sail you regulate the watch to the local tide tables, then you can tell at a glance exactly how many hours it is to high tide, to low tide; it shows the period of strongest current, and is built to run on the average semi-diurnal sun and moon cycles time.

Electronic compasses and brilliantly designed sailing-performance computers, showing windward performance and the ratio of reaching performance, can also be bought.

When you buy any electronic equipment check carefully what is its accuracy, how it is covered by guarantee, what servicing is provided and available; what is the *full* cost (does it include installation and spares?).

It does teach one to appreciate the courage and navigation of the young Airas Tinoco, of whom I wrote in the beginning of this book, when one realises how much help we have to navigate, and how little he had.

STORMS

Don't go to sea if you dislike getting wet. Apart from giving you a cold bath, a storm is unlikely to harm you if you are a moderately good sailor. Admittedly, sea water does possess unique powers of penetration, and in rough weather often seems to get through unnoticed chinks in clothing.

Kenichi Horie sailed safely through a typhoon in his tiny plywood 19 ft. boat, but he is exceptionally good.

Between the *dialogue of the wind and the sea*, as Debussy called it, there is nothing to shelter a man and his boat; as nowhere else one can perceive the enormous power of God. Chay Blyth wrote: *To atheists I say, go sailing singlehanded for a few weeks*.

A storm calls forth specific qualities, particularly presence of mind. Never lose your temper in a storm; the sea and the wind will not listen, your crew if any have enough to worry

THE BEGINNER'S GUIDE TO SAILING

about, and never lose patience with yourself. I'm not denying that a few well-chosen epithets won't help to relieve your emotional strain. However inept one of the crew may seem in a moment of crisis, don't expect to treat him as did the mariners who cast Jonah into the sea, that was a special occasion.

The power of the sea is incomprehensible to a landsman; *At midnight I was at the tiller, and suddenly noticed a line of clear sky between South and South-West. What I had seen was not a rift in the clouds, but the white crest of an enormous wave. During 26 years experience of the ocean in all its moods I had not encountered a wave so gigantic.* (Sir Ernest Shackleton, 1874-1922. *South*).

In the *Roaring Forties*, it is nothing to encounter waves a ¼-mile high, and round the Horn, much higher than that. Yet boats and their men survive.

If you go sailing in an estuary or out to sea do make a *habit of listening regularly to radio weather reports and forecasts, before setting out and while at sea.*

One thing to learn to do well is to hold on, and railings, lifelines (essential for lone yachtsmen) are a must. *He fell, and lost the helm from his hand; and the fierce blast of jostling winds came, and brake the mast in its midst, both sail and yardarm fell far down into the deep.* (Homer's *Odyssey*).

In fact most modern boats are better built than ancient craft, and technique is so advanced that many men know how to save their craft and their lives by a jury rig (emergency substitute mast, made from any broken spar or piece of wood, and any bit of sail or cloth rigged up to catch the wind). With this emergency in mind, always carry some tools for repairs, etc. Saw, grips to splice wire cables etc. Nor forget that you might have to replace the rudder. Beware of what type of metals you use (screws, etc.) because the action of seawater on some alloys is disastrous. Sir Francis Chichester was in the Roaring Forties when he found that a winch supplied to his boat had been made of the wrong alloys, and the metal had seized together in one, solid, immovable mass!

Do get your gear from a good, reliable, long established chandlery; your life is worth more than the saving of a few small coins.

Don't eat greasy food before a storm, but if you know one is approaching get something hot to eat and drink, and if possible, put some hot cocoa or similar beverage in a vacuum flask, and store it where it cannot roll out and break.

When you set out make sure that your well-wishers at the bar or on the quayside were sailors themselves, and if they are *stout mariners, disturbed and anxious, levelling their glasses at the sea from behind places of shelter, as if they were surveying an enemy* (as Dickens wrote), do take their advice, however much it may run contrary to your wishes.

Writing particularly for solo yachtsmen, the great Adlard Coles said: *The yacht in 9 cases out of 10, can look after herself, and in the 10th case you may need your strength, which is why reserves should not be frittered away.* Another authority, Captain F. H. L. Searl, put it this way: *More troubles arise at sea from the failure of the human element.* So *keep warm, keep calm, keep alert.*

Do not worry about the boat, she was built to take it. Never let the noises of a storm distract you. Noise is only sound. And do not spend time waiting for a storm reading accounts of great voyagers' efforts during a tempest. Enjoy those only during a calm or when hove to. Imagination can make an approaching storm seem much worse than it really is.

If a storm has been forecast lash down everything movable. Batten down the hatches. Make certain the valve of the marine toilet is closed. Check the strainers of the self-bailing cockpit, make sure they are clear. Have storm jib and trysail ready for use if you think you will need them, and probably you will.

Learn to estimate the effect of different wind forces on your boat. The reactions differ according to the length, beam, draught, area of sail carried, etc. Often the worst damage a storm does (other than to your emotions) is in the cost of what it smashes (loose gear), rips (sails), or washes overboard. Otherwise a bad blow may do little more than show you how efficient, watertight and snug your boat is, and how good a sailor you've become. *In a storm one comes to know the good pilot* (Giovanni Verga, 1840-1922).

No two storms are ever alike, and it is not practical to give specific instructions on how to behave; only general rules and ideas can be given.

You have heard a forecast or have noticed some weather signs that indicate that a storm is coming. Decide whether you have sufficient speed and take a chance on arriving safely at a harbour *only* if you know that harbour, know how to enter it, know the local tides, and if there is no bar before it. (Entering harbour at ebb tide during bad weather is dangerous. The entrance to a harbour can become a swirling whirlpool during a storm.) If not, keep out of harbour, and away from the shore. Above all avoid the peril of a lee shore, the end of good boats and incautious sailors. The rocks and boulders on the shore will do more irreparable damage to a boat than the sea will. In *The Brassbounder* is a description of the yachtsman's ultimate horror: *Faint as yet against the sombre monotone of sea and sky, a long line of breaking water leapt to their gaze, then vanished as the staggering barque drove to the trough; again, again, there could be no doubt. Breakers! On a lee shore!* (Captain David Bone 1874-1959).

At all costs every effort must be made to claw your way into the wind off, away from, a lee shore. Better than making this difficult effort is to ensure that you don't get into the position of having to try it.

You are safer at sea in a storm than in running for the shore. On a broken coastline it may be possible to find some shelter to leeward of a small island where you can heave to.

A small cockpit is less trouble than a large cockpit during a storm, and any boat destined for coastal, estuarine or seasailing should be equipped with self-baling equipment, and should have two bilge pumps, one of which is working inside the cabin; all strainers should be kept clear, cleaned regularly and accessible for clearing during an emergency, debris, sand and seaweed can impair their efficiency.

You may find it possible to use the power of the storm to your own advantage, as did Gilliatt in *Toilers of the Sea* (Victor Hugo, 1802-85), but know your boat and know your storm before you take risks.

Basically, if the boat runs faster than the stormy sea the waves will swamp her. *If a boat runs slower than the sea she*

THE STRESSES MOSTLY EFFECTED BY STORMS

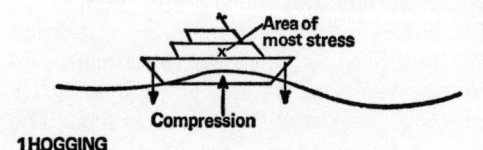

1 HOGGING

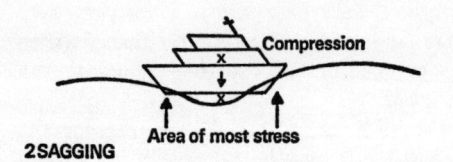

Area of most stress
Compression

Severe when midship is compressed and the ends are unsupported

2 SAGGING

Compression
Area of most stress

The ends are held between the trough

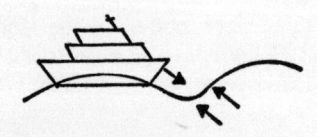

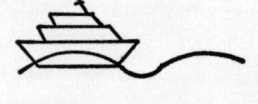

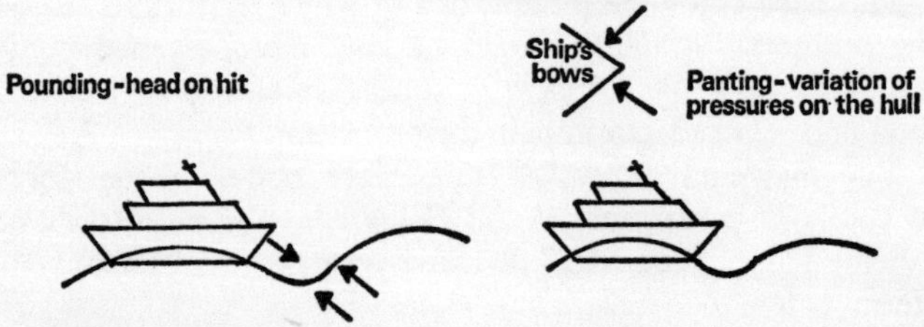

3 PANTING & POUNDING

Pounding - head on hit

Ship's bows
Panting - variation of pressures on the hull

STRESSES ii

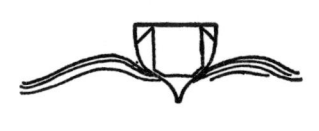

i Normal

ii Badly heeled

Damage to transverse section

4 PACKING

i
This is swinging broadside on into the trough. Apart from making the craft difficult to handle it produces transverse stresses

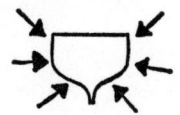

ii
Possible forces of stress

5 BROACHING

A DANFORTH

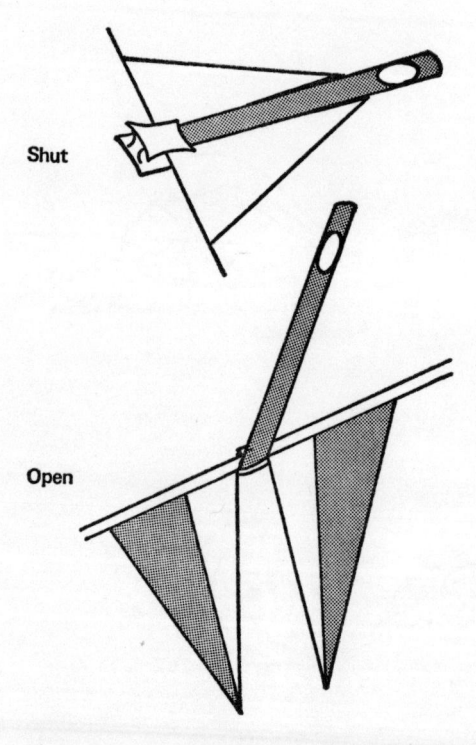

Shut

Open

This anchor will hold a yacht up to force 10 (maybe more) but beware of violent change of wind direction, with sails up, the Danforth might loosen and drag

will ride the waves. To slow a boat down use warps with anything heavy attached. An anchor (e.g. Danforth or a special sea-anchor) towed 5-6 fathoms with a warp and tripline often suffices to slow a boat down, especially if you are running

THE BEGINNER'S GUIDE TO SAILING

for shelter (leeward of island, headland, etc.).

Make certain that you keep a firm grip on the warp and the trip line; lose either and the apparatus becomes virtually useless, so fasten them round a cleat.

If a yacht cannot show a good reaction to her helm there is less benefit from the long warp and sea anchor.

You may decide to lower the mast in its tabernacle (after lowering sails), then if you lash your helm to leeward, with the benefit of a Danforth or sea anchor warps you may find it safe to ride the storm. This will lessen heeling, but will still allow some rolling (you can't win 'em all).

In all fairness I think I must agree with the opinion that a ketch or yawl are more comfortable for riding out in, because of the balancing effect of a small area of sail at the mizzen mast. Many sloops and cutters have ridden out and conquered terrible conditions, but after such catastrophes tell it not in Gath. Some amateurs have forsworn the sea and taken up chess instead; it is not everybody who likes his stomach being bounced up into his throat at every pitch and roll a sloop makes in a storm.

One advantage of riding out a storm is that it gives you and your mates time to get hot food and drink (provided your cooker is on gimbals, and it certainly should be). This is better with a long keel boat than with a short keel; the latter allows you to drift, sometimes totally out of control. In a storm bind rags round the warp where it is likely to chafe against the fairlead; movements in a storm could burn the rope otherwise. A violent sea may work screws loose in anchor shackles, and it is helpful to strengthen these with wire.

Never let your yacht lie broadside to the oncoming waves, however difficult this may seem. Many famous solo yachtsmen have reported that in some storms (force 9-12 particularly) the waves seem to be coming from all directions at once.

As a general rule it is not wise to heave to if the wind is force 8 or above. If it is above this and rising, and depending upon how much water you are taking on board (a storm wave may represent *tons* of weight rather than just gallons of water) your best chance is probably to run for it. Some small

EMERGENCY SEA ANCHORS

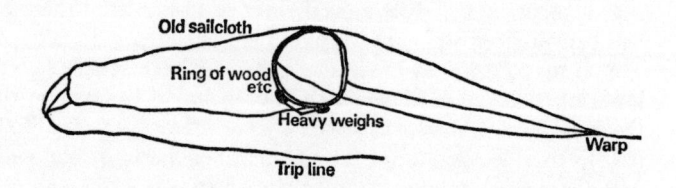

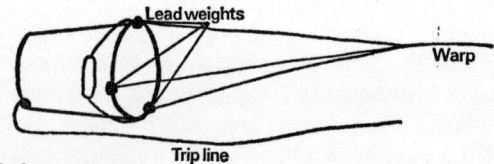

Old sailcloth
Ring of wood etc
Heavy weights
Warp
Trip line

Lead weights
Warp
Trip line

Plastic bucket with its bottom bashed out

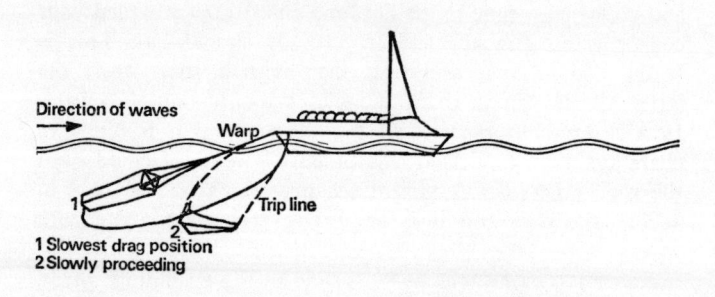

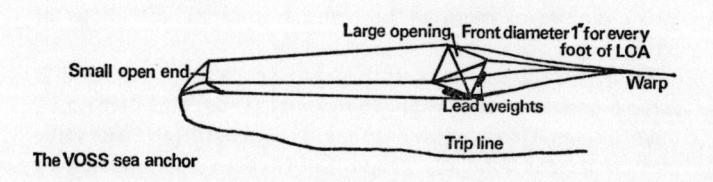

Direction of waves
Warp
Trip line
1 Slowest drag position
2 Slowly proceeding

Large opening. Front diameter 1" for every foot of LOA
Small open end
Lead weights
Warp
Trip line

The VOSS sea anchor

craft have survived bad storms by lowering all sails, lowering the mast in its tabernacles (if you can) and relying on buoyancy and water-tightness to see them through, on the basis that the less resistance offered to the wind the less likely one is to be destroyed between the wind and the waves battling it out.

All of this information is relative to the size of boat and the sailors aboard. Whereas 16-year-old Robin Lee Graham could set off round the world on a solo voyage, very few yachtsmen twice his age have the experience afloat he had *before* he sailed on his epic trip.

You can ride to a sea anchor or run with it. Many believe it is better to have the boat's stern towards the oncoming direction of the waves. In which case a canoe or counter stern is quite a blessing. But if the craft has sharply cut-away bows they are not so efficient when riding at anchor. Every advantage of boat design is balanced by a disadvantage if conditions are encountered that are other than those it was designed for. What makes you faster in racing will be inconvenient when cruising etc.

If you are running or reaching in rough weather, using a storm jib or similar; it is a safe bet to put a steadying line through the clewcringle, then if the wind should veer, or the sea turn violent and rip the sail, or snap the sheets holding up the sail you won't lose that sail. Aboard a ketch or yawl there would most likely to be a small sail on the mizzen mast as well, and the same rule applies.

It is always a bit of a puzzle for the beginner to know where to go when he knows a storm is blowing up, but there is one piece of information which has its origins in the dim past. North of the equator you sail for north or the west, or northwest segment of the storm. South of the equator you sail for the south, west or south-west segment of the storm.

From your burgee or a ribbon tied to a stay, note the exact direction of the wind. Face yourself to the wind. Stretch your right arm out sideways, then put it one hand's width further back behind your shoulder; this is now pointing approximately to the centre of the storm.

Having identified the centre, allowing that the prevailing wind is from west to east, work out whether the boat will

ROUGH WEATHER CANVAS

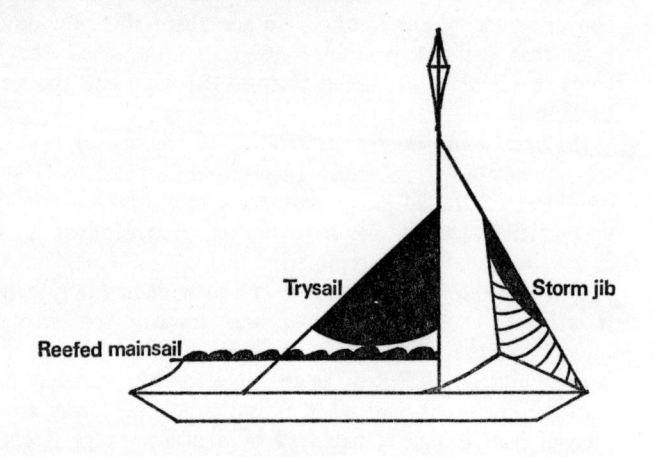

Trysail — *Storm jib* — *Reefed mainsail*

be hit by the northerly or southerly part of the storm; go to the directions indicated according to your position above or below the equator.

SAILS DURING A STORM

Rule 1 is this: Make certain that the sail your boat carries can be handled by the crew, whether there is one of you or a dozen.

Rule 2. Never have a trysail that is heavy and awkward to handle, because it will seem twice as clumsy during a storm as during practice in port.

Rule 3. Water has the power of a very solid force; a large wall of it can tear a sail from the mast. Judge carefully how much sail you show.

Rule 4. If you have a ketch or yawl remember that the small sail aft helps to balance the ship and makes it easier for you to keep a good weather helm.

Rule 5. If the wind is blowing up, but you are running, ostensibly to get away from the centre of the storm, but your boat's rail is being forced down to wave level, take in both reefs (see above), and use a small storm jib.

THE BEGINNER'S GUIDE TO SAILING

Rule 6. Practise reefing, and make sure you can do it quickly and efficiently on a calm day in harbour, then on a calm day off shore; if you force yourself to practise a little *before* you encounter *weather*, during a storm it will be just as easy to do (apart from wearing a lifeline, gusts of wind and an excess of spray and water).

REEFING

We will start with the easy bit. Some modern yachts are being provided with roller reefing, by which the main boom (and mizzen if there is one) is unlocked from one position, and then, with halyard loosened, you simply roll the boom round, stretching and smoothing the sail to *avoid creases*. This decreases the area of sail challenging the wind, and makes the craft more manageable. When you have judged how much to take in, you push your boom back into the gooseneck (which holds it) and it will keep locked again. As a general rule it is better to reef too much than not enough—try taking in as far as the lowermost batten on your mainsail (remove batten!). Reefing should be practised during calm weather, and practised so often that, like a guitarist who need not look at his strings to play, you can perform quickly and efficiently. From *Midshipman Easy* I take this piece showing the speed with which reefing may have to be done:

The sky which had been clear in the morning was now overcast, the sun was obscured with opaque white clouds, and the sea was rising fast. Another 10 minutes and then they were under double-reefed topsails, and the squalls were accompanied with heavy rain. The frigate now dashed through the waves, foaming in her course and straining under the press of sail.

illustration overleaf.

GENERAL NOTES

A small forestaysail has often been found more useful than a storm jib. Generally speaking, storm sails are of heavier canvas to give better resistance to tearing, and have tough bolt ropes; they provide slow movement but help keep the

REEFING BY POINTS
As opposed to modern roller reefing

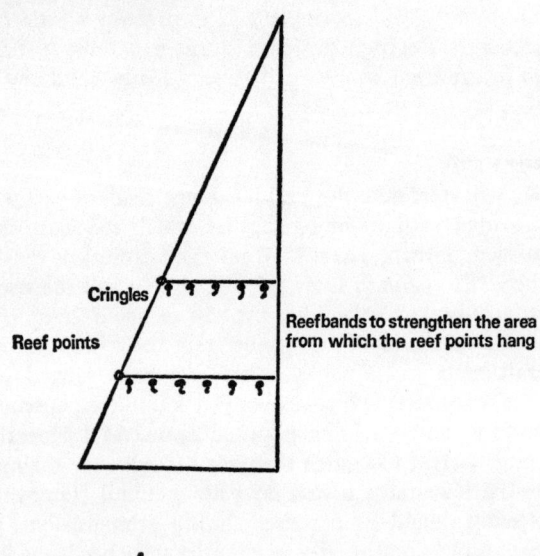

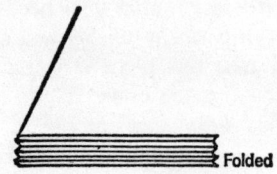

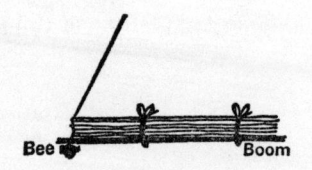

Cringles

Reef points

Reefbands to strengthen the area from which the reef points hang

Folded

Bee   Boom

BERMUDAN MAINSAIL

ship in *your* control. The trysail, most usual with Bermudan rig (rarely gaff) usually has a loose foot.

MOTOR-SAILERS AND THE LIKE IN STORM CONDITIONS

The sail-less power boat is at a disadvantage during a storm because without a sail it can use up so much fuel battling against the waves, trying to maintain its planned course that it has none left to get to the desired port. Every boat venturing to sea, even on a short coastal jaunt, should carry one or two sails.

Power boats are usually fair-weather boats, and although they can make an impressive spray-scattering scud for harbour before a storm becomes more than a menace on the horizon, they are, because of their different design, nowhere nearly so safe once a storm has broken.

The owner of a boat that has no sails had better heed the advice given by the liontamer's son ('Don't go in the lions' cage tonight mama'): Let us look at it this way—with a wind force 8, waves can reach up to 25 ft. and the wave speed can reach 34 knots. With a force 10, the waves reach nearly 40 ft. In bad conditions the wave speed can go over 40 knots. Admittedly these are the approximate maximum figures, but they are good enough insomuch as nobody knows when a sudden squall may whip up to the worst storm in living memory. The sea is totally unpredictable.

If you are caught out everything that can slide, slither, fall, crash or spring out must be lashed down. Pump the bilges as dry as possible; they will fill up again, have no fear. Get a fix on your position, check the time, mark these in the log. Get the warps and sea anchor ready (if you haven't got them with you start reading your Bible, you're going to need a lot of prayers).

If there is time after these preliminaries get some hot cocoa inside you, and maybe a bite to eat, prepare some sandwiches or rolls, and more hot drinks (store the thermos flasks where they will not fall out and break) because you have no idea when you will be able to get a proper meal again; a storm that is a long time coming lasts longer than one that comes up suddenly.

For a short time the rudder is useless in the air, just long enough to yaw

Make sure the life-lines are fastened to you and some solid part of the ship. I hope your boat has grab rails and plenty of firm parts to hold on to, above and below decks; it should have.

Now for some hints on what you may do.

1. Never slam into the waves and force your way against a gale to reach your home port when there is another haven where you may ride out the storm near at hand. Life and the boat may be at stake. A storm can turn really vicious in a matter of 15 minutes.
2. By turning the boat to meet the seas about 30° you can reduce the angle at which your boat will roll about. If you meet the sea at right angles your roll will increase threefold!
3. Generally speaking, above wind force 6, do not try to use your speed to overtake the waves, you can get trapped in the trough, yaw violently and capsize. This sort of thing adds unnecessarily to the struggles of the man at the wheel or tiller. Going flat out can leave the rudder high and dry while the unhappy boat is at the mercy of the direction of the crest of a wave.
4. It is usually safer to keep steerage, slow down, stream warps behind you (more than one probably), sea anchors and all. Use the fenders (old tyres) etc. to make the warps slower.* Although this will not stop the drenching effect of the water surrounding you it is safer in the long run. You can get dry later!
5. Whether your boat has a mast or not, you can use some part of the structure to run a stay to the transom, and run up a sail aft which will help the sea anchor to keep your bows facing the wind. The sail should be sheeted in taut. If it flaps it won't help much.
6. Avoid trying to turn the ship when you have warps astern; a sharp turn might bring about capsize.

7. If you are in estuarine waters keep over to the weather shore, the wind will keep you off that, but go to the lee-shore and the rocks and mud may damage you more than the waves.
8. Keep the rule of the road even during a storm; a sailing dinghy tearing across your bows may be less able to control herself than you to control your craft.
9. If you are lucky enough to have reached harbour, be careful how you enter it during storm conditions. If you have enough fuel left you can make a run for it in the trough of a wave, but try to keep an eye open for following waves that might slap you mercilessly into the harbour walls. Do not try any sharp turns on entering harbour, the cross movements of the swirling waters can capsize you.

Lastly, keep calm, think ahead, and remember you are not the first of the breed of men to be in a storm.

Hammocks are easier to sleep in during a storm than bunks, because they swing with the motion of the vessel, and the sleeper stays relatively still.

No doubt after a storm you may echo Dickens's Mr. Tapley, *any land will do for me after so much water!*

The man I met who most enjoyed storms was a customs officer in Spain; he it was who got me to read Pierre Loti's *Iceland Fisherman*; he revelled in passages such as: *Lashed to the helm, like caryatids, they only moved their numbed blue hands, almost without thinking, by sheer muscular habit.* He lived in Torla in the high Pyrenees, and had never been to sea; still I thank him for a wonderful lunch, and some very good trout fishing.

FOG AND MIST

When fog is approaching *check on the chart* what your position is, this is *most* essential.

If you are near any shipping lane, get out of it *quickly*.

---

* Old petrol, cans, floorboards, planking, furniture, anything you have can be fastened on to a warp, but make sure it is really fast!

If you are run down in a fog your friends can't even wave you goodbye, and as Ulf and I used to sing: *auf einem Seemans Grab da blühen keine Rosen* (No roses grow on a sailor's grave).

Use echo sounder to get the most careful soundings possible, or the simple *leadline* (don't sneer at this old-fashioned device, it never breaks down at a crucial moment as does some electrical equipment!). Old salts call out leadline depths as 'Mark ten', 'Mark twain', etc. The author Samuel Clemens adopted the latter as a pen name, after hearing this called out by boatmen on the wide Mississippi, and as *Mark Twain* he became world famous.

Foghorn signals must be made according to the requirements of Rules to prevent Collision. Do not flatter yourself that if some super ocean liner runs you down you will get compensation. By the time the company's landsharks (lawyers) have finished you will be selling your salvaged craft to pay for their scratched paint! If you heave to you are still required to make foghorn signals. During a fog the navigation, if you do not heave to (which is not always advisable), must be by dead reckoning.

Beware of sound in fog, it is always distorted by the moisture in the air, and there are pockets of inaudibility through which sound does not penetrate, so that out of the eerie silence can come a bellowing horn as some liner moves down upon you if you are in a shipping lane. Radar, radio-direction-finding, and similar equipment all make the finding of one's position very easy now, so if you go out beyond the coastline you must have such equipment aboard. The indefatigable compilers of nautical almanacs, amidst millions of other facts, find time to compile neat lists of radio beacons and all the call signs they use. A radio telephone link to shore is luxury indeed, and makes navigation easier. *As a general rule, slow down and keep going slow during all fog and mist conditions.*

Although navigation lights are not 100% effective it is often wise to use those in a bad fog, in case other shipping has strayed off course. The golden rules of fog navigation are two: *Know your position,* and *make sure others know it from your signals.*

GONE AGROUND?

This frequently is a result of faulty navigation during fog or mist conditions, less often, it is caused by bad navigation in sunlight. Nearly everybody goes aground at some time during their sailing career so don't sit there blushing; see what you can do to work yourself loose.

It is easier to run aground under power than under sail because the screws will chug merrily until you are deep in the mud when they will disobligingly stop, and often refuse to do anything even in reverse to get you off. Your first move with power is to go into reverse, but slowly, because the water pump or jackets of the cylinders could get choked up; it is usually advisable to shut the power off and try to get free without it. The *Danger Sign* for going aground when under power is *if the wake shows sandy or muddy water*; stop engines at once, use a pole, boathook etc., and check the depth, punt yourself round, reverse and get away from that spot. If you are nearing shoals under power always keep one eye on the wake your screw turns up.

Another simple trick is to cast your anchor out over the stern, as far as you can throw it, and then, everybody taking a hand, you try to haul yourself off by brute strength, don't give up too easily.

Most of these measures also apply to sailing craft without power. If you are unlucky enough to go aground on an ebb tide, you may not have time for the finer methods, and the only alternative to staying there uncomfortably and waiting for the next flood tide will be for one or two of the stronger crew members to go overboard, flounder around in the mud and push you off (of course, if it is just one man and a pretty girl aboard you might as well give in and wait for the next flood tide). When a boat runs aground it carves a niche for itself in the mud. By rocking the boat from side to side (all crew members stand on one side until she begins to heel, then over to the other side, etc.) it is possible to widen the niche until the boat can slide out of it. Again, if all crew members go astern and exert their weight there the fore may rise gracefully out of the mud and you can slide away. If all crew members but one get overboard a small boat will often rise up without further ado: This is a cold and wet

AGROUND

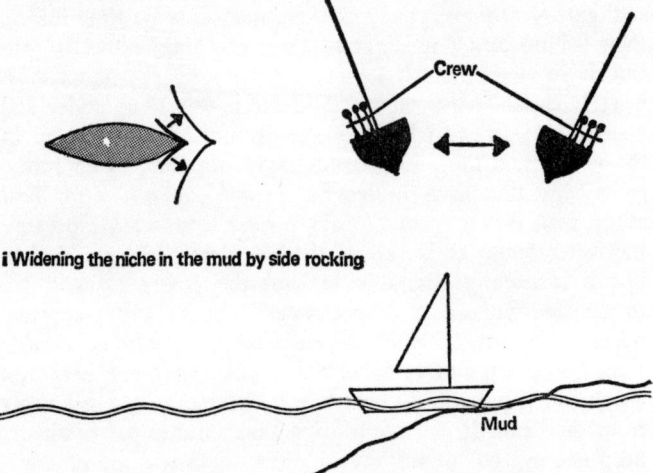

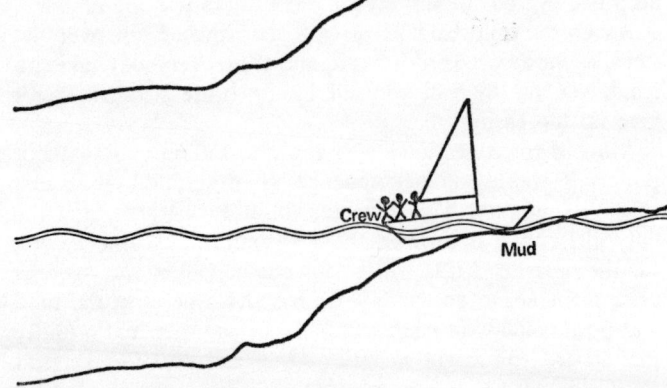

i Widening the niche in the mud by side rocking

ii Sliding free by stern rocking

solution. If the tide is rising, row out by inflatable dinghy or what have you, and drop your anchor in deeper water as far out as chain allows, and as soon as the tide begins to make her move a little, pull in on the anchor chain and you'll be free. If you have a *centreboard* craft, the first and obvious solution is to pull up the board, when you will most likely float.

The worst way to go aground is when there is a neap tide. Then your craft could be stranded for 12 to 14 days, but if your navigation is up to average and you avoid wholly uncharted waters, and take care to keep to reasonable channels, this shouldn't happen to anybody.

Safety Check List

If your boat is 18 ft. LOA or less you should consider carrying the following:

1 lifejacket of approved specification for each person on board.

1 or 2 lifebuoy(s) and 100 ft of buoyant line with a breaking strain of 250 lbs.

1 main anchor with sufficient cable for mooring in the type of waters you expect to visit.

1 spare anchor and between 60 and 100 ft, of line for it. Especially useful if you are fishing.

1 good bilge pump, and don't forget to have a bailer or old plastic or rubber bucket attached to a line, tied down somewhere handy.

Compass; a sea mist can come upon you with no warning at all.

2 distress signals of approved flare type.

First aid kit, and, if you have an engine, tools for repairs to it.

2 oars (although harder work they are often safer than an auxiliary engine).

A torch is always useful.

If you know you are going out of sight of land regularly a transistor radio is a good apparatus to have with you.

1 fire extinguisher is especially necessary if you have an engine and useful just in case the cooking gas gets spilt.

If your vessel is longer than 18 ft. then in addition to the above items you would be wise to take either a dinghy or an inflatable on voyage with you.

You would normally carry 2 or 3 fire extinguishers (instead of one) depending on whether the ship was 30 ft. or longer.

You would then carry six distress signals instead of 2—two of these should be of rocket parachute type.

HOW MANY IS A SAFE NUMBER

Well, if your boat is 12 ft. LOA she should not carry more than two people, 14 ft will take 3 people, and 16 ft. and above will take 4.

For coastal and estuarine work it is seldom wise to go out far in less than 18ft. For a longer sea voyage in deep water you need at least 24 ft. and maybe 30 ft. with a beam about one third of the LOA. Basically, it depends upon two factors —how good a sailor you really are (not what your friends tell you when they want a free trip) and how much room you need to live in; the smaller the boat the more cramped you feel on a long voyage.

Collision: Rule of the Road at Sea

International regulations have been agreed upon to help prevent collision and disaster at sea.

The following is a simplified version of the rules.

Visible, this means that a light must be normally capable of being seen on a normal dark night with no mist.

With reference to blasts, short is of 1 second duration, and long averages 5 seconds.

1. Power-driven vessels require on the foremast or on a forepart of the ship a *white* light giving an unbroken arc 225° of the horizon (10 compass points on each side of the vessel). It should be visible up to 5 miles. A stern light is also carried; see the note below.
2. On the starboard a green light is to be shown giving an unbroken arc of $112\frac{1}{2}°$ (10 compass points); it must be visible for 2 miles.
3. On the portside a red light is shown, the same arc and visibility as the light specified in 2 above.
4. Normally the green and red lights are fitted with screens to prevent the lights flashing across the bows and causing confusion.

    Note: A sailing vessel does *not* use the white lights (1) *ever*, but she does carry one white *stern light* with a visibility range of not less than 2 miles, giving an unbroken arc of 12 compass points, being visible $67\frac{1}{2}°$ *each side* to port and to starboard astern.
5. Craft of less than 40 ft. are normally required only to show the starboard and portside lights with 1 mile visibility range (but if you expect to be in coastal waters or offshore in deep water, near a shipping lane, that 1 mile would hardly be enough).
6. White lights, visible for 2 miles each, are usually required for any vessel which is at anchor, although only a fore light is insisted upon; the use of a stern light may also help avoid collision. During daytime larger vessels especially are expected to display a metal black-painted ball sign if they are at anchor.

WHISTLE A HAPPY TUNE

One of the most beautiful sounds of the sea is the music of foghorns and whistles answering each other during a rising mist.

Power-driven craft moving ahead sound a long blast every 2 minutes.

Power-driven craft not moving ahead sound 2 long with 1 second interval in between, repeating this every 2 minutes.

Sail moving ahead 1 blast when going on a tack to starboard. 2 blasts when going on a tack to port. 3 blasts if wind is abaft her beam. All blasts in quick succession.

Aground, a vessel may ring a bell for 5 seconds at a minute interval.

STEERING TO AVOID COLLISION

If two sailing vessels approach each other in conditions that might allow of a collision the rule to follow is this:
(i) If the wind is on the same side of each vessel the ship to windward keeps away from the ship to leeward.
(ii) If each ship has the wind on different sides the vessel with the wind on her portside must keep away from the other ship.

If the vessels are driven by power the procedure is even simpler—each alters course slightly to starboard, thus passing port-to-port.

The full details can be obtained through any sailing club, and should be studied before you go into crowded sailing waters or on coastal and sea voyages.

Remember that nearly every stretch of coastline is liable to have some local rules, and inquiries should be made locally for these, particularly in fishing areas.

Technically, steam (power) should give way to sail; in current practice this does not happen enough, sometimes because the power boat is going at such a speed that it cannot possibly stop or take avoiding action in time.

There is a note about the rule of the road under the heading for *Dinghies and Racing*.

Inboard Engine Check List

Most of us pay more attention to the inboard engine when it is sick. Here is a list of common symptoms and the prescribed treatments.

1. Engine turning, but no start.

   Out of petrol. Plugs or ignition damp. Defective coil. Dirt or water mixed with petrol. Distributor points burnt. Leak in petrol pipe. Condenser damaged or punctured. Air vent and overflow choked. Ignition switch or wiring faulty. Fuel pump not working. Distributor rotor burned up. Carburettor loose on your manifold. Broken wiring. Vapour lock. Distributor points loose.

2. Engine going but boat won't go.

   Propellor damaged, jammed or loose. Coupling or shaft broken. Out-of-adjustment manual gears. Too little oil in hydraulic gear.

3. Engine going, then stops.

   Battery gone flat. Overheating. (Often low octane in high spark setting.) Check all points listed in 1 above.

4. Starter will not turn.

   Battery terminals too loose, dirty and clogged up. Wiring loose or broken. Starter defective, examine the button or key. Solenoid out of action. Battery going flat.

5. Starter does not make engine rotate.

   Solenoid faulty. Drive faulty. Dirt, water or oil in cylinder. Battery flat, or nearly so.

6. Starter motor turns but engine won't.

   Solenoid induction faulty. Drive faulty.

GENERAL NOTES

A breakdown always seems worse in coastal or deep waters, but keep calm. Drop anchor, unless you could drift safely in closer shore with the tide helping you; then you could row in the runabout for help when near enough. A two-way radio was built for such emergencies as this; if you've got one use it.

Keep your petrol clean; don't store it in some dirty old can you developed a sentimental attachment to 40 years ago! Water is not good for petrol-consuming engines, they drop dead at the first touch of it. If there's water in the tank, you will probably have to drain the lot out (do not throw it away, it can be treated) and start again. Check for any loose part admitting air to the system (will clog the fuel pump).

One much neglected point is to keep battery connections clean and *greased*.

Always check for rust in any engine at the start of the season after a winter lay-up; a thorough overhaul in the spring can save you a lot of trouble.

Remember that going aground may result in mud or silt clogging up the water passages of an engine's cooling system!

A final warning. Petrol left all winter in some old tank will partly evaporate, and may form silt deposits with chemicals on the metal. It will also lose some of its advertised octane power.

OUTBOARD MOTORS

Generally speaking, the carburation, ignition, water circulation and oiling are much the same as for inboard engines. The checking for faults is also much the same.

When an outboard is frequently in use always check the mountings of the engine on the transom; make sure they do not get worn down and so change the angle at which the engine operates under water (cavitation).

It cannot be emphasised too much how important it is to clean and dry the engine thoroughly before storing it away for the winter.

Never leave your outboard engine lying carelessly on the bottom of a boat. The speed with which it can rust, absorb dirt, and deteriorate has to be seen to be believed. These are expensive toys, to say the least, and a wise man will build some rack to hold the engine, upright preferably while it is onboard but not in use. Keep it in a rack when ashore.

An engine that is left on a shed floor or on a pile of junk will soon be nothing more than a pile of junk.

When not in use keep the engine covered from dust, dirt and damp. Salt water may corrode the outer casing.

128   THE BEGINNER'S GUIDE TO SAILING

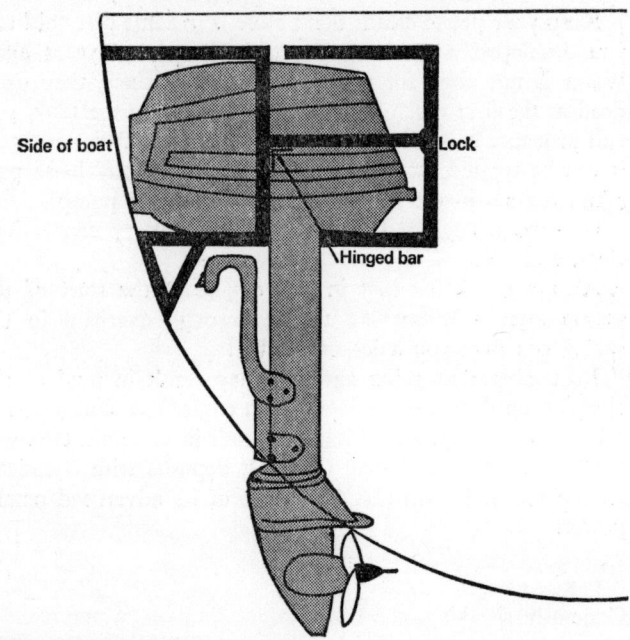

One style of RACK for an Outboard Engine

Never skimp on the oil the outboard needs. When the oil supply is correct there comes a faint blue, almost invisible, haze from the exhaust. If the exhaust shows up white and voluminous there is too much oil; drain a little off.

Never use a cheap grease for the lubrication; it may go hard in cold water and cease to function properly. Last year's old grease is this year's poison to your engine; remove it and replace it.

Do not go slow for long periods; in some engines it can soot up the plugs; when you buy the engine the seller should provide you with a manual about it; this will indicate what speeds are the most efficient to run.

An outboard needs to be kept clean much more than an inboard does. It is usually advisable to wash off salt water with fresh water. If the engine is dropped in the sea you may have to drain out the fuel tank, feed pipe, carburettor,

calm voyage.

Friends about to race.

Keep your balance!

cylinders, and clean movable parts with petrol before greasing, oiling and reassembling—it depends on the make.

Remember that the propeller must be deep enough in the water to get a proper purchase.

One more piece of advice which can save you a lot of money—do listen more to the builder of your boat than to the salesman for the outboard manufacturers; you cannot always better speed performance by getting an engine with larger horsepower; the boat may not be designed to give you more than $4\frac{1}{2}$ knots! Anything else would take and waste more fuel with no appreciable results.

Beware of automobile engines converted by an enthusiastic amateur for marine use; in many cases you would be better off carrying a second pair of oars!

Maintenance and Repairs

Care saves the expense of wear should be the motto of those who go down to the sea in ships.

SAILS
Never allow your sails to dry out while reefed, especially if they are artificial fibre sails; they are very expensive to replace.

Sails are carefully made to curve out in the right places; I know of one or two cases where the sails have cost as much as the yacht!

Crinkles and creases will ruin their effectiveness. You can't iron them.

If damp or wet nylon sails are stowed away they will stay creased.

Aim at letting your sails hang loosely in a drying wind while moored.

Never dry sails by electric heaters.

It is invariably cheaper to have sails properly washed by a sail laundry; this will get the salt and grime off, and they will come back dry.

If your sails are furled, keep them covered with a waterproof protector.

Do remember to repair the sails before washing them; if the damage is bad it will be cheaper to send them to a proper sailmaker for repairs.

Check batten pockets; the edges tear easily.

The battens may need varnishing or renewing.

Check cringles and seams for rents.

Check the luff wires of foresails.

Some stains, and light mildew, can be removed by using 1 part of bleach to 10 parts of water (beware if using on coloured sails).

HULL & TIMBERS
Use fresh air and sunshine to keep your boat free of dry rot and fungoid diseases of timber.

Timbers should be cut out and replaced, by an expert, if damaged by rot or diseases. Do not accept cheap offers; it may mean that the wood being used has not been properly seasoned, and this would only increase your expenses later.

When the repairs are dry use several coats of marine paint.

Use anti-fouling against *gribble* and *teredo* worms.

Always inspect and dry out your bilges; they are a constant source of trouble if not dried out.

Remove and check ballast.

If you can afford it copper sheathing is an excellent preventative on the bottom of a ship.

In the early stages of infestation sailing a week or two in fresh water and then a week or two in salt water will kill off most marine worms, because those who prefer the one water cannot live in the other.

Get barnacles, weed and salt layers off and hose down and dry the hull before inspection.

Check the rudder/tiller, transom fittings and fittings for the outboard motor.

Check the centreboard and its housing. Spray with anti-fouling.

Examine the keel for damage.

Check garboards (next to the keel) for worms; spray them with anti-fouling.

Look at the caulking, canvas or deck covering; if it is no longer fully waterproof you will know it too soon.

If painting or varnishing, remove all dust, grime, and salt, get the timbers bare to the wood before opening your tin. Minimum 3, preferably 4 coats are advised. Polyurethane paints and epoxy coatings have lasting effects. Read the manufacturers' instructions before painting.

CABIN & GALLEY

Check, clean and where necessary replace sleeping bags, mattresses, hammocks, carpetting, linen, cutlery, cooking stove, gear, saucepans, etc.

If laying up, remove all good gas bottles (canisters).

Clean out and dry out the water tanks.

Check the sea toilet, check its valves for efficiency. Drain off water.

Engine: Check batteries, magneto, etc. Drain off petrol.

Remove clocks, compass, all easily movable gear that might tempt prowlers if you are laying her up over the winter.

Never leave an outboard motor in the cabin during laying up.

Laying up afloat may be more practical for a timber boat, because a 10 or 12 week lay-up in dry dock during the winter may split her timbers.

Check the fire extinguishers (you should carry at least one).

Check the buoyancy bags, life jackets, etc.

MAST & RIGGING

The golden rule is: Never leave a mast lying on the ground when ashore or while laying her up for winter; it will cause distortion by warping, and strains are possible even in metal masts; they are not built to stay long in a horizontal position.

Check all movable gear, pulleys, winches, tackles, and clean them of dirt, grime, salt and verdigris.

Check the gooseneck carefully for wear.

If you have roller reefing gear check it carefully.

Check shrouds, stays, and luffwires of foresails (bend the wire in a few places along its length; if a strand snaps you may expect the others to go soon, replace it—the cost is cheaper than the price of a new boat; furthermore, upon such a slender thing your life could depend.

Check halyards, eyes, shackles and replace any that are worn.

When examining the halyards attach sufficient line so that you can draw the halyards back down a hollow mast more easily.

The threads of bottle screws may have worn loose, which means you could lose sails, rigging, even the mast, during a storm; it is cheaper to replace the bottle screws.

It is a good idea to rinse the sheets in warm water to get rid of the salt. Dry them carefully and naturally (no electric heating): Replace them if worn.

Clean and check the efficiency of all running rigging and blocks.

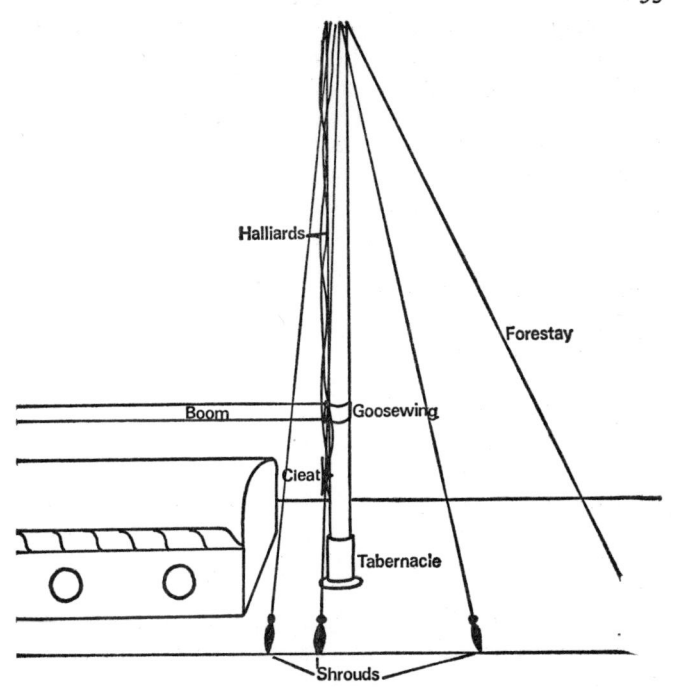

Figure labels: Halliards, Forestay, Boom, Goosewing, Cleat, Tabernacle, Shrouds

Clean and grease pins and sheaves.
Do label all rigging before storing it up for the winter.

GENERAL

Clean mould, mud and weeds from the anchor at regular intervals.

A mud berth is often kinder to an older wooden boat; the dampness of the mud prevents the splitting of drying out timbers.

If you have your boat hauled out by a yard you *must* make a full inventory of every item aboard; hand 1 copy to the boatyard, keep 2 copies for yourself (you might need one for the solicitor if open disagreement develops).

Accompany the foreman of a boatyard, check over with him everything to be repaired; get it in writing. 99% of boatyards are honest, but you could have picked the other 1%!

Check that the boatyard is using full-strength anti-fouling; if it is thinned down it is useless.

If you want to work on the inside yourself, arrange this in advance with the foreman.

DINGHIES—Special notes

Check the toestraps, if they failed at the wrong moment you could lose a race.

Remove bungs, ensure that air can circulate freely if the dinghy is laid up under canvas, plastic, etc.

Do take care to support keel and bilges evenly, otherwise warping may ensue.

If the mast is unstepped be careful that it is properly supported to prevent warping; never leave it lying on the shore.

Almost any trailer-borne craft can be stored on a rack, keel uppermost.

It is not essential to store in a garage or shed during winter but it *is* essential to ensure ventilation during the lay-up.

GLASSFIBRE—Special notes

It is essential that GRP and similar craft made of artificial combinations should be properly supported while laid up ashore, because there will be severe pressure damage to their lines if left badly supported during the winter.

Do not use powerful chemical cleaners and abrasives, but just lots of soap and water which cannot damage the top layers that would lead to invisible damage, cracking and general internal deterioration below the surface.

Check for chafing on plastic of centreboard housing.

Very great care should be taken not to use caustic strippers on woodwork or sometimes on plastic surfaces.

Cover and ventilate during laying up. Some of these craft may absorb nearly 2% of their weight in water if neglected: this may mean losing a race because it would slow you down.

LAST WORDS

Boats are expensive, the longer they last the less the cost to you.

The more you care for them regularly, the longer they will last.

When Nelson was dying he is reported to have said: *Thank God, I have done my duty.*

Caring for your ship comes under the heading of duty.

HITCHES, KNOTS AND BENDS

A *hitch* is used to fasten a rope to a spar or any other object. The first illustration shows a *half-hitch*; it is rarely used alone. More familiar is the *Clove hitch*, popular to shut tight a duffle bag, etc; it tightens as you put a strain on it.

The *Rolling hitch* is a development of the *Clove;* it is more secure than that, adding just one ordinary turn between the clove.

Clearly recommended for any anchor is the hitch named after it, illustration p. 136 shows how it is tied.

The *Shore hitch* is useful for a long-term mooring, but 'getting hitched ashore' is a slang term for a man who uses his shore leave to marry his girl (quite understandable as long as he doesn't desert his boat).

The *Spar hitch* is used for hoisting a heavy spar or load aboard ship. Add a half hitch at the end if a stopping effect is needed.

A knot is a turn or series of turns in a rope twisted to make the rope fast to its standing (strain) part, or to fasten some objects securely together.

One of the toughest and most popular of sailors' knots is the Bowline, and it is used (with the *Reef*) probably more than any other knots.

Never use a *Reef* for tying two separate ropes together; it won't hold, its name came from reefing the sails.

If a rope is worn thin and can be shortened, use the *Sheepshank* knot and make sure that the weakest portion of rope lies between the two terminal areas of most strain.

Fishermen use the *Bloodknot* frequently, it is useful for thin line, and especially for holding a slippery line secure.

HITCHES

i HALFHITCH

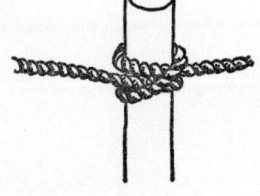

ii CLOVE HITCH

iii ROLLING HITCH

iv ANCHOR HITCH

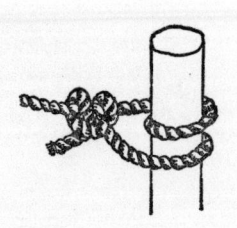

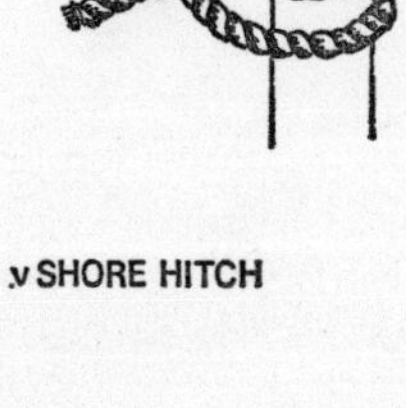

v SHORE HITCH

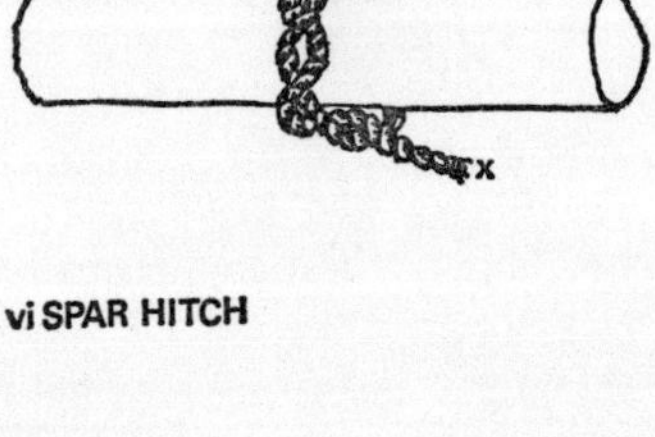

vi SPAR HITCH

THE BEGINNER'S GUIDE TO SAILING   137

KNOTS

vii BOWLINE KNOT

viii REEF KNOT

ix SHEEPSHANK

x BLOOD KNOT

xi EIGHT KNOT

E*

It is often useful to give a rope a stopper so that it does not slip or run, and for this purpose an *Eight* knot is commonly used; as the illustration shows a simple 8 is easy to make.

A *Bend* joins two rope ends together; this is a form of ropework that, used carelessly, could be a fatal mistake. If you have to join two ropes, do not improvise something, use a bend which you know will work.

The *Sheet, Double Sheet, Hawser* and *Carrick* are all illustrated here. When you throw a light line ashore for some friendly type to heave in your hawser and fasten your boat to a bollard you fix the light line to the *hawser* cable with this bend.

The Carrick is used for hauling, towing, for cables and very heavy anchors, etc. It can be knocked open by a belaying pin, and doesn't need a marlin spike (which can damage a rope) to undo it.

Many books on sailing can dishearten the beginner by discussing dozens of knots, hitches, bends and splices, most of which one can buy from a chandlery, already made, unless one has time to spare to spend a few hours making them. In modern sailing, especially when different sheets are often made of coloured artificial fibre ropes, the knowledge of ropework the average week-end sailor requires is less than it was a century ago.

A chair-leg will serve as a spar for practice, and by consulting the diagrams you will learn more easily than by reading a text; it is better to sit down and look at a picture than to work out complicated wordy explanations. Gnarled ancient mariners have been wont to instruct their young apprentices with such detailed explications as: *See 'ee 'ere, this is 'ow it's done*.

If you enjoy ropework and want to become an expert in the field there are many manuals all about it; remember that the bit of rope fastened to something or taking the strain is called the *standing* bit, and what is left beyond a knot is called a *fall*, and to make really knowledgeable the curled over loop is called a *bight*. When you have got your teeth into that, get an experienced man to show you how he does it, and learn the 15 knots, hitches and bends shown here until you can do

THE BEGINNER'S GUIDE TO SAILING 139

BENDS

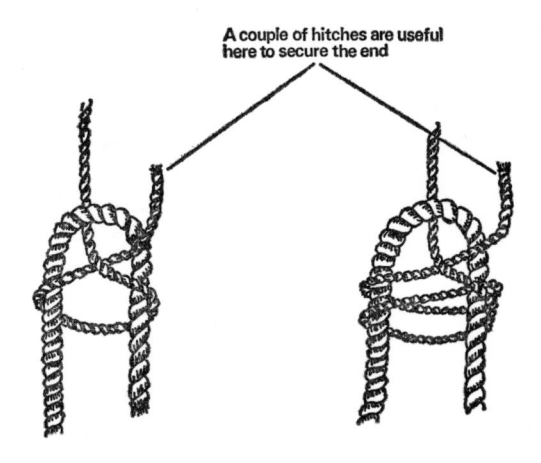

A couple of hitches are useful here to secure the end

xii SHEET BEND

xiii DOUBLE SHEET BEND

xiv HAWSER BEND

xv CARRICK BEND

them all quickly, easily and correctly without any reference to the book.

May all your ropes hold good, and your knots all go without a hitch, if you'll pardon the expression.

Clothing

Ever since the days when Erik the Red discovered America, and Snorri Sturluson wrote the *Heimskringla* (12th C.) men have had to learn that the sea is no respecter of persons. It is one thing to read Boyd Cables' inspiring words about *the taste of the scudding spray, sharp and strong and salty on their wet lips,* but to sit shuddering and shivering with icy dollops of water sluicing down your neck because you forgot some essential item of clothing is another thing altogether.

Unless your idea of boating is a 110 ft. floating gin-palace, from which you may occasionally catch a glimpse of the sea from the plastic and chromium equipped bar, it is wise to pay very careful attention to the clothing you wear at sea, and take to sea . . . or indeed upon any waters.

All clothing for sailing should be designed for comfort, warmth and practical use.

To start with, particularly if you are a novice, avoid a white peaked cap; these are more popular among taxi-drivers and bookies than mariners. (If you are starring in a movie about sailing but not intending to get wet a white peaked cap is good for shading your eyes from the arc lamps.) If you look around any harbour the men in jeans, rough pullovers, woolly hats (which have seen better days) and look like derelict hulks at ebb-tide have probably done remarkable feats of sailing, things such as a solo round the world, a trip round Cape Horn, or hold an ocean-racing cup; one or two of them may well be a *Sir* to boot!

If a pretty wench comes aboard in stiletto heels you have two alternatives—either to throw the shoes overboard before they ruin your deck surface (cracks that could let gallons of water into the hold during some storm you decided to sleep through), or throw the girl overboard; with those heels she would only trip and fall overboard in shark infested waters, so you would save her the agony of waiting for it.

If a man comes aboard with an umbrella that is unlucky for seamen, so either turn him back before he commits the sacrilege or trip him off the gangplank. Some fish will eat anything.

If you are seagoing take two extra pullovers, as well as the one you are wearing when you set out. You will need at least one extra pair of jeans because it is uncomfortable going ashore in a pair that are soaked through with spray and salt. I advise three extra pairs of thick (Norwegian) socks. All that gear should be stored in two waterproof bags, one inside the other. If you are doing some river, lake or estuarine cruising you could make do with one of each of the items, stored in one waterproof bag only.

As to underwear, handkerchiefs, etc. you would reckon these as if for any other holiday. String underwear, commando pattern, is definitely best.

A good warm shirt is practical (regardless of sex), but nylon or artificial fibre shirts are useful only for shoregoing.

For top-gear plastic coating over the fabric is useful.

In sailing parlance the outermost layers of clothing are classed simply as *Oilies*, from the days when they were made of oiled cloth. For comfort the boat must have a locker to hang them up to dry off; one where the drips will not run down your neck while you are cooking hot cocoa on the Calor-gas.

If you venture to coastal, estuarine waters or right out to sea the oilies should be yellow or orange, the safety colours that are easiest to see at a distance.

WHAT TO BUY FOR OILIES

You have a simple choice, fashion does not enter into it. You can either buy cheap oilies that will need replacement every second or third season, or a dearer set that may last 4 or 5 seasons. Their life depends on the frequency of use, length of time worn, and, especially, how many storms they have weathered.

PVC is popular but it cannot stretch easily, and becomes brittle when it ages. Nylon or Terylene and plastic-coated materials, are liable to crack if exposed for long periods to the extremes of heat and cold one can all too easily experience at sea. There are times when it seems nothing is completely impermeable.

NEVER carry more aboard than is absolutely necessary and NEVER take an umbrella aboard ship – unless you WANT her to sink!

If you go to sea or on coastal work, you should wear a lifeline with some harness round your body, especially if solo.

If the weather begins to look nasty, fix a length of an old towel round your neck, like a scarf; it will save you from several trickles of water down your spine if you wear it under your oilies.

If you begin to feel tired, bad-tempered or shivery, or even very talkative, remember these may be *exposure* symptoms, and take care to get wrapped up, something warm inside you, and if possible some rest.

If your gear has zip fasteners on it, grease them lightly with lanoline cream, Nivea, etc.

Kenichi Horie, sailing the North Pacific, used many pairs of cotton gloves, and threw these and his used underwear overboard during his trip; he had, (wise lad) an aversion to washing clothes at sea.

In racing it is becoming popular to wear a one-piece suit; these let in very little water indeed, and as anyone here can see, racing is a wet business altogether.

I prefer the French-style plastic sandals for sailing. Rope-soled and several other types of shoes pick up too much sand, mud, grit and small stones as you come back from being ashore, all of which damage the deck coverings.

Never wear wellies or ankle-length boots; these are very difficult to swim with, and if you never visualised the prospect of a sudden unexpected swim you shouldn't go sailing. If you can't swim, consult my *Beginner's Guide to Swimming and Water Sports*.

SAFETY CLOTHING

Every country has regulations about lifebelts, jackets, etc. You should always be sure that every member of the crew has a jacket of approved standard before doing coastal, estuarine or sea sailing. The basic principle is that the jacket, when inflated, shall support an inert, semi-conscious or exhausted person slightly backwards so as to keep nose and mouth free for unimpeded breathing; the angle suggested is about 50° inclined rearwards, head leaning over backwards. The apparatus shall be such that the person wearing it can swim, as well as float, comfortably.

Preferably it should be capable of drying quickly and easily, and strong enough not to rot if immersed in water for long periods.

Always practise putting the jacket on several times during the season, whether you need to or no. Always wear it if racing or cruising in sea, coastal or estuarine areas, and in bad weather anywhere. The front and the back of each jacket should be clearly marked for immediate identification.

STORES—WHAT TO TAKE WITH YOU

Every home should have one . . . Firstly, what any boat could need: Adjustable spanner, metal saw, wood saw, pliers, screwdriver, pins, safety pins (large size, *not* for nappies), cotton rags or waste, line, oil (especially if you are carrying outboard or inboard auxiliary engine), shackles, line and twine, bailers (rubber ones do not scratch fine woodwork or damage artificial resin surfaces), a bilge pump (maybe two in a cruiser). Try always to have a really good seaman's knife to hand, and a few plastic pails, bowls, buckets, etc.

If you expect to be away from your moorings for three hours or more take an anchor with you (preferably two) and 80 foot of warp or cable etc. for each anchor. A mist could come down suddenly; within 20 minutes everything in a familiar estuary could become a sinister blob in a pitch-dark world; perhaps your best chance of safety would be anchoring, so this is not the time to remember that you left it in the club locker or the garage.

The *golden rule*: Take what is necessary in preference to what is less so, and do not be over-influenced by articles in glossy magazines that could be thinly disguised puffs to sell you something a true sailor would be less likely to need than his mother-in-law aboard ship.

If you expect to sail beyond coastal or estuarine waters out into the *wine coloured seas* as Homer called them, you should expect to take more gear with you. Definitely two anchors, maybe three, and three times the quantity of warp or chain for each anchor (240 ft.), foghorns, lights for navigation, fog and to avoid night collisions, safety equipment must be carefully checked aboard, fuller first aid kit is needed, spare sails, spare rigging and stays particularly, and as much twine and line as you have room for—it always comes in handy sooner or later.

Be sure that you keep sailbags dry and clean; look after them as well as you would the sails; if the bags get damp they will ruin sails too!

Flares and signalling equipment generally, according to estimated needs. If you are *going foreign* you will need insurance papers and documents proving ownership of the boat.

Fuel oil and spares for an auxiliary engine are also essential.

Tools for repair of engine.

Cleaning pastes to get engine oil and dirt off hands before handling those gleaming white sails.

Navigational tables, pilot books, charts, sextant, compass, dividers, tide tables, nautical almanac (interesting reading if nothing else) a telescope or binoculars are among *my* list of essential items.

Well, you will say, this is all very well, all that is for the boat, what about me? Put it this way, if the boat isn't properly equipped you will end up only a memory, the boat comes first, sorry!

You will need oilies (nylons or plastics), spare pullovers, change of clothing, towels (an old towel used as a loose scarf when on watch is good to keep your neck sprayproof and handy for other emergencies), plenty of woollen socks, toilet paper (don't tear pages out of the Nautical Almanac), life jackets, a couple of lifebelts, a torch (with batteries), matches to light the stove (keep them in some waterproof covers) and plenty of fuel—whatever your cooker burns. And as much *fresh* water as you need. I assume that the ship is permanently equipped with fenders, sails, barometer, etc. It should be.

FOOD

Take more than you think will be needed for the journey, in case you are stranded, becalmed or run aground for a turn of a tide.

If you take camera and film carry both in two distinct water-tight plastic bags, then only the camera and binoculars if there is a strong strap to hold them round your neck, in case the ship gives a sudden lurch while you are using them.

FIRE-FIGHTING EQUIPMENT

Is essential if going on a trip where there will be cooking or lighting by combustible fuels (i.e. other than electricity). A fire far out to sea is a terrible but usually avoidable disaster.

Health, Hygiene and Diet

I personally prefer herbal first-aid to man-made chemicals, as readers of my *Concise Herbal Encyclopedia* will know. In that and several other books on the subject I have detailed the natural substitutes which one can carry instead of artificial pharmaceuticals.

I invariably have some tincture of myrrh, witch hazel, eucalyptus oil, slippery elm (internal upsets), tincture of marigold etc. with me. Castor oil and olive oil, are, of course, both herbal products. Everybody should have a few roller bandages, triangular bandages (and perhaps a first aid book to tell you how to tie them), gauze and lint for dressings. Plenty of Elastoplast and adhesive tape, tweezers, safety pins, a thermometer, a scalpel for digging out some deeply-embedded splinter etc. Some cascara sagrada tablets (in case the cooking constipates you), you may think quinine tablets useful (herbal products again), and if you expect sea-sickness any of your favourite antidotes for that. A large bottle of brandy, for medicinal and other purposes, is often kept in the medical stores. Of course, thousands of men go to sea for a weekend without carrying any of these things, but it is useful to foresee dangers and be prepared rather than regret a tragedy a little bit of care could have avoided.

If you get constipated (no motion of the bowel for 48 hours) you are much more likely to suffer from sea-sickness.

Coldness, wetness and greasy food also contribute to sickness. Keep away from the smell of any auxiliary engine, eat dry food, keep in the open air, and, if you can, do something to take your mind off your stomach.

I would tend to place oil of peppermint immediately on a burn, bandage it up and keep it clean; a sterile dressing could be used dry instead.

If somebody is too near the stove and clothing catches fire wrap them in a blanket or anything that cuts off the supply of oxygen to the flames. Flames out first! Otherwise there will not be anything left of the person to attend to.

If going to sea for a weekend or longer do try to take some

fresh green vegetables with you. There are many forms of cooling (polystyrene boxes) etc. that olden sailors never had, so there is no need for you to fall ill with some of the diseases which are a direct consequence of a lack of fresh green foods.

In my *Beginner's Guide to Swimming and Water Sports* there is a detailed and very simple account on how to save people from drowning and resuscitate those who have been in the water and are more or less unconscious. You should keep the book handy, and learn the techniques well.

Keep warm! Beginners often fail to notice how cold the evening at sea is getting until it is too late. It is your duty to others and yourself to keep well during a sea voyage, but don't expect others to do the job for you.

INSURANCE

Unless you are of the feckless and reckless kind, like H. de Vere Stacpoole's *Sea Gypsies*, you would be strongly advised to insure your craft.

The world of insurance is poorly charted, there are hidden shoals, and many a poor sailor has found his end there. I hope the following words may be of some help.

Insurance salesmen always look kindly folk, and are frequently able to produce, with the speed of a shifting wind, a highly impressive document that may easily blind one with science. It often offers you protection against piracy, but the last pirate was hanged a century ago, and the modern concept of piracy is the stealing of a ship on the *high seas* or the seizure of its cargo, so whether this impressive clause applies to the owner of a 12 ft. dinghy is doubtful. Another promise is to reward the policy holder if he suffers from barratry, which means a fraud worked by the master of a ship against the owner—since you are probably the master, owner, pilot, cabin-boy and crew any way, this is not much use to you. I have seen policies that guarantees a ship against earthquakes, but not against hurricanes—judge for yourself which is likely to be most likely at sea. *Make sure the policy covers what you want.* Firstly, make sure there is cover for theft; this usually demands that you accept responsibility for reasonable care of the craft, locking cabins, hatches etc. If negligence is proved against you the contract will be invalid. The policy should

INSURANCE

PIRACY?

OR SINKING IN A STORM?

Does your Insurance Policy cover you against REAL risks?

cover sails and equipment stowed aboard *when at moorings* as well as when sailing. Personal gear, clothing, cameras etc. may be an extra charge on the policy; ask about this.

Make certain that the policy covers you against loss by fire.

Storm damage should be covered so that if you lose your sails during a gale you get *new sails to replace them*.

Collision and damage to the other boat as well as your own should be covered by the policy. It is important if you have an auxiliary engine to make certain the engine is covered by the insurance. The cost of spares and parts will usually be covered, *but not the labour* to install the same. The loss of an outboard engine is usually covered only by paying an extra on the premium. If an outboard is stolen, and it is shown that you made a habit of *not* locking it up or placing it in a position of safety, there is little likelihood of you receiving compensation. Sand or silt in the engine is usually a risk covered by policies which include the engines, as is stranding due to those causes; but check before you sign whether the cost of a tow (incurred because you were aground and could not get off) is specifically included; it should be.

Make certain that if you move out of an area specified by your contract that you are covered by the policy. I.E.: Your policy may specify that it covers river or estuary cruising, if you wish to go on a coastal cruise for a week, phone the company and check with them (get confirmation in writing) whether you are covered; maybe a small extra will be required, but it *is* worth it). If it is not convenient to inform them beforehand, drop a card or note to the company in the post, say where you are going, and sign that you will pay any extra premium required when you return; give the time and date from which cover is needed.

You may expect some reduction in the premium to be paid if you accept some of the following clauses:

- Specific definition of an area of sailing; river, coastal, etc.
- If your boat is incapable of more than the 15 knots.
- If it is moored at a recognised boatyard, club or marina where there is some supervision.
- If laid up during the winter months, either afloat or hauled out. (N.B. The cost of hauling out, lifting out, etc. may

exceed the saving so be careful, your boat may not require an annual overhaul.)
- If it is a registered yacht (easier to trace in case of theft, etc).

POSSIBLE EXTRAS
- Racing may need special coverage for sails and spars.
- Dinghy or rowboat carried may need a small extra payment.
- Hauling on a trailer behind your car (if it's that size of boat).
- Delivery to you by the seller from port to mooring must be covered by your insurance once you have paid your deposit, unless specifically covered and confirmed in writing that it is covered by the seller's insurance policy.

WARNINGS
Most policies clearly indicate that they are void if the owner neglects the reasonable care of his boat.

If somebody carelessly leaves the valves of a sea toilet open, within an hour a storm blows up, and down she goes. The company will soon find out that the valves were left open, and all the expenses of recovery etc. will be yours.

Dry rot, and neglected repairs may also invalidate a claim.

By and large, deal with big well-established companies, it is cheaper in the long run; if the claim is just they do not quibble about it.

Be fair and shipshape in all your dealings with them and they will do the same by you. You may find it advisable to deal with a company handling business for several yachtsmen in the district. The locals will tell you the pros and cons, and the company will realise that careless handling of a claim could lose them more than one man's business.

On joining a club

Apart from the social advantage of being able to exchange experiences, advice, gossip and so on with the other members there are many advantages to be had from joining a yachting club. The trouble is, in any country, there are so many, so which one do you join, and how do you make the choice?

Firstly, analyse what you want to do—racing, cruising or just pottering about in boats? If it is racing make certain that your choice does race the class of boat you own (or are about to buy), because you don't want to get involved with transatlantic yachts if you have a 14 ft. dinghy—or vice-versa.

Be sure, secondly, that the club has got moorings if you need them, and provides facilities for lowering a trailer into the water if you take the boat home with you and bring it down at weekends.

A third point to look out for is whether the club provides (itself) or has a chandlery nearby; it can be frustrating if you are in urgent need of a bit of rope or chain to find that the nearest supply is 50 miles away; it may mean you miss a tide.

Connected with the last point is the fourth—facility for repairs. This may or may not include cranes and gear for lifting out a boat at the end of the season, but it should include sufficient space for you to do some scrubbing down and a bit of hammering, painting and pasting of resins, etc.

Lastly, but not leastly, the prices at the club bar for drinks and refreshments might give you a good idea about the sort of clientele they get (regardless of what the club secretary may tell you). If they are *normal* then the members will be; if they are over-inflated prices, you will know what to expect of your fellow members.

Of course, no yacht club has perfect access from the road; well, none that I have known, any way, but they have perfect access from the water, and rarely can you have benefits both ways.

Don't join a club unless you are prepared to get dirty helping a fellow member do something that no one man can do alone, if you can't join in to pull on a rope, lend your shoulder to support something etc. If the members aren't prepared to do the same for you, clear out, find another club.

Bibliography

(i) Books about voyaging which I can recommend:
   Kodoku: Kenichi Horie.
   Dove: Robin Lee Graham.
   Impossible Voyage: Chay Blyth.
   Sailing Alone Around the World: Joshua Slocum
   Voyage of Gipsy Moth IV: Sir Francis Chichester.
   Riddle of the Sands: Erskine Childers.
   Offshore: John Illingworth
   Ulysses Found: Ernle Bradford.
   The Sea Around Us: Rachel Carson.
   Cape Horn: Felix Riesenberg.
   A World of My Own: Robin Knox Johnston.
   Kon Tiki: Thor Heyerdahl.

(ii) Sailing:
   There are a large number of works on sailing by the following authors, all of whom write very well:
   Peter Heaton, F. H. Searl, Maurice Griffiths, Adlard Coles, Uffa Fox, Ian Nicholson, etc. etc. Any library would help you if you ask for the titles. Most of these authors have written several books on the subject.

(iii) Technical, Charts, etc.
   Works such as Reeds' and Browne's Nautical Almanac, Pilots Books for specific areas (telling you how to enter a harbour, avoid dangerous currents, submerged wrecks, etc.) and charts of oceans, seas, estuaries, etc. can all be found easily on application through a yachting club, a public library, or by application to the authority which is in charge of navigation in a country. Invariably official charts are cheaper and more reliable than others.

Glossary of Nautical Terms

In the following section numbers given refer to Chapter(s) in which there is a *significant* reference to the subject. For many words no number is given because it is not considered essential. Occasionally alternative spellings of old nautical words are found (i.e. *halyard* and *halliard*) and I use the most authentic known to me.

Most words are of Anglo-Saxon or Viking origin, where possible this is given in brackets at the end of the definition.

OE—Old English   ON—Old Norse

Aback	Sail pressed backward on the mast by the wind, the sail being held by sheet to the weather side (*on bæc* OE).
Abaft	Behind (*bæften* OE).
Abaft her beam	Bearing beyond 90° from straight ahead.
Abeam	At right angles to the line of your boat (*on béam* OE).
Aboard	On or in a ship (*on bord* (the side of a ship) OE).
About	To go about is to tack on the opposite side (*onbútan*, on by outside OE).
Abreast of	Side by side in a straight line with (*on bréost*, breasts in line OE).
Adjustment	Pieces of metal inserted into the compass to counter the alterations effected by local disturbances to the needle's magnetism. 8
Adrift	Being driven away, broken off from moorings, usually out of control (*drifan* OE)
Afloat	In a condition supported by the water (*flóta* ON, *flotian* OE).
Aft	The back part of the ship, by the stern, go aft—go to the back (*æftan* OE).
Aground	On the ground, not afloat (*grund* OE). 8
Ahead	In front, at the head of the boat, directly in line with the bows (*on héafod* OE).

Alee	The shout *hard alee* tells us to put the rudder to the weather's direction side as far as we can. The shout *helm alee* tells the skipper that the tiller is now to leeward (same as *helm up*) (*á hlé* ON).
Aloft	Any height above the level of the deck. To go aloft is to climb a mast (*loft* (sky) OE).
Alternating Light	Light for navigational guidance, showing alternating colours, the pattern of which is specified in the pilot book for the area. 10
Amidships	In the middle of the ship, lengthwise or widthwise. A rudder held amidships is in line with the theoretical lengthwise direction (*on midden* OE).
Anchor	Any implement that keeps a ship by chaining it to the bottom securely. A sea anchor is dragged to slow a ship down (*ancor* OE). An anchor buoy is one linked to an anchor to warn you against fouling across it. An anchor light is a white light visible from any angle to warn other shipping that you are at anchorage.
Anti-cyclone	An outflowing of air in a rotating fashion from an area of high pressure, usually associated with good weather. 7
Anti-fouling	Any paint or substance that hinders marine creatures from making a meal of your boat. 12
Apparent wind direction	Your boat is sailing merrily on a course, the burgee or ribbons show the apparent wind between your direction and the true wind. 7
Astern	To the rear of the boat or behind that.
Athwart	Across, athwartships being from one beam to the other (*thvert* ON).
Avast	Stop, hold fast there (*Houd vast!*—Dutch).
Awash	On a level with the water, at the mercy of the waves.
Aweigh	The anchor is just being raised from the bottom.
Aye aye	The standard form of saying *yes* at sea. It comes from the correct English *yeah* from OE *géa* (German *ja*), the word *yes* comes from a

	Norman-French form meaning *I hear you*.
Back	See *aback*. If the wind *backs* it changes anti-clockwise in its movement.
Backstay	A support that links the masthead to the stern. Running backstays can be adjusted but go down to opposite fastenings on either side of the boat abaft.
Bail	To take water out of the interior of a boat, done with a *bailer* which is a bucket or whatever serves the purpose (*bejgla*—a bent scoop ON).
Ballast	Fixed ballast is usually attached to the keel, while shifting or movable ballast is just in the hold or bilges of a ship. The object is for the heavy weight of ballast to balance the ability of powerful winds to overturn the vessel (*bar last* ON).
Bar	A bank or shoal found at the mouth of a river, harbour.
Bare poles	Sailing under b.p. means without sails set.
Battens	Stiffening pieces of wood or plastic inserted into the pockets on the each edge of a sail to keep its shape. 7
Batten down	The meaning of the word relates to a thin plank of wood, and those planks that were fastened over open hatches when a storm was expected. Possibly related to the word *béatan* OE. 8
Beam	*Béam*, the side of the ship, the length of the tree (as in horn*beam*) that goes to make up the vessel's side. Thus the width of a boat, in measurement the widest part. Also a position that is at 90° to the middle of the line running fore and aft of the vessel.
Bearing	You are looking at an object, its direction from you is read off on a compass; this gives you its bearing. 8
Bear away	To sail away from. To move away from the weather.

158 THE BEGINNER'S GUIDE TO SAILING

Bear down	To sail straight on to a point. To sail with the wind.
off	To leave moorings, etc.
up	To sail away from the weather. To sail towards—to bear up on.
Beating	To make one's way against tide and wind, to sail straight to the windward, done by tacking (*béatan* OE).
Becalmed	The wind has dropped, you have no engine, you are becalmed!
Becket	A loop of rope with an eye at one end and a knot at the other. From the old Dutch word for a bend of rope.
Beeblock	A block of wood attached flat to a spar (e.g. boom) so that a line can be led through it, for reef ropes which fasten the sail to the spar.
Belay	From the OE *belecgan*, meaning to twist a rope around to hold it fast, this is done with figure of eight twists round a cleat (or bollard ashore). If rope that is knotted gets soaked with rain or spray it is impossible to untie quickly. Hence the custom of belaying. A belaying pin is a piece of wood (movable) that can be used for belaying a rope round.
Bells	The old custom of mariners before portable electronic watches were available was to sound bells by number to indicate the passing of time. One Admiralty notice announced: *as from the 21st of this month sunset will be at 8 bells! How omnipotent can one get?* Needless to say the term sunset was a judicial one rather than the real thing.
Belly of the sail	The full part between the edges, that which billows out.
Bend	To fasten a sail to a spar and make it ready to hoist. To bend is also used for fastening a line on to something (*benden* OE—to bind together).
Bight	A small bay on the line of the shore. A loop

in a rope, made without a knot. Sometimes used of loose rope (*bugt* ON).

Bilge — This is related to the word *bulge*, and is the curved, full part of the ship below the water line, hence the whole of the lowest part of a ship; the water that collects there is called bilge water, and the rubbish, sweepings, etc., are bilge. From the OE *Bælg* also comes the word bag. Bilge keels, fixed to the keel of a small yacht, increase her lateral resistance to windward and help her stay upright.

Binnacle — Casing in which a compass is housed, usually with lighting. The word is of Portuguese origin, and refers back to the days when these intrepid mariners began man's discovery of the world.

Blanket a ship — To take the wind from another craft to leeward of you.

Block — A pulley with a wheel (or several) in it, giving a safer purchase on something hauled through it.

Boom — This is the old Dutch word for a tree; it means the spar that accommodates the foot of a sail, the mast to which it is attached gives it its name; main, mizzen, etc. Since tree trunks can be used for many purposes it is not surprising that the markers showing a narrow channel through mudbanks, shallows, etc., are also called booms.

Bosun's chair — A plank-like seat worked with pullies and slings to haul a man up a mast for repairs. The bosun or boatswain comes from the ON word *sveinn*, meaning young man; it is more suitable for a younger than an older one.

Bottle screw — Commonly used to alter the tension on standing rigging. There are two threaded pins which are drawn together or eased apart.

Bow — From the OE *bóg* meaning shoulder, hence the shoulder of a ship, the front end of the boat: The bows are the sides of the same. The bowsprit is a spar extending forward from the bow

	so that a stay for foresail can be fastened there.
Break ground	You sail up to the anchor or loosen it from the ground by hauling in its warp or chain.
Broach	To turn sideways on to the waves and the wind, often in the trough of a storm wave. This often resulted in one of the early ships breaking up, OE *brecan*, to break. 8
Bulwarks	Sides of a ship rising above deck level. (Old German).
Burgee	A small pennant or club flag.
By and large	Sailing with the wind slightly off the beam.
By her lee	When the wind veers round so that it comes on the same quarter as your boat has got her mainsail. 7
By her stern	Boat trimmed deeper aft than for'ard. *By her head*—vice versa.
Cable	200 yards (one-tenth of a nautical mile) or 100 fathoms in depth. Also any thick rope, especially that of an anchor used of chain as well as of rope. The word is Middle English.
Capstan	An upright appliance by which a cable is wound on board.
Careen	To put a boat on her side to expose normally submerged parts for scraping and cleaning etc.
Carlings	Timbers that go between the beams.
Carried away	Broken off during a storm, particularly of spars, etc.
Carry helm	When there is a marked wandering off course over a continuing period of sailing the helm is used to correct this, and the ship is said to carry helm.
Cast off	Throw off mooring ropes etc.
Catspaw	First indication that a gust of wind is coming, seen by the pattern of movement on the water. Also the hitch in a rope that can provide two loops, for a hook, etc.
Cathead	The beams by the side of the bowsprit through which the anchor cable passes, hence the use of *cat* for anchor. 7
Centreboard	An extremely ancient discovery, still popular.

	It enables a boat to have the advantage of a keel when sailing but to retract it when mud-hopping and in shallows.
Chain plate	A metal fitting to hold the deck end of shrouds.
Chart	A map of water (and what lies beneath it etc.) coasts and harbours are shown with much useful information on tides, lighthouses, etc. etc. 8
Clawing off	A boat that is trying to force her way slowly off a lee shore (in a storm) and get round to windward. 8
Cleat	This is a metal or wooden fitting with two prongs, round which ropes may be secured, from the OE *Cléat*.
Clevis	A metal pin with an eye drilled one end, through this another pin is passed to hold it steady, used to secure rigging, etc. OE *Cliwen*.
Clew	This is the lowermost corner of a sail's after-edge, where the leech meets the foot. Also from OE *cliwen*.
Coaming	The built-up woodwork around hatches, etc. to prevent water going down; often more effective in theory than fact. Possibly from OE *cumb*.
Cockpit	Sheltered lower part of a yacht's exterior. Of ON origin.
Companion	Stairs or ladder aboard ship. Probably of *Dutch* origin.
Counter	The part of the hull that lies back of the stern post.
Crab (to)	To stall with an oar in the water by getting the wrong rhythm if feathering it across the water (See my *Beginner's Guide to Swimming and Watersports*).
Cringle	This is a loop worked into the roping of a sail, as head, clew or tack. Of OE origin.
Crown	That part of a traditional anchor where the outstretched arms link to the main stem.
Cuddy	A sleeping place or cabin of a small boat. OE origin. (Compare German: *Kajute*.)
Cutting	A tide between spring and neap.

F

Daggerboard	Of Middle English origin, it means a small keel or retractable small centreboard.
Dead reckoning	Quite alive in fact, it means, a *ded*uced estimate of the ship's position, without use of sextant, using just tide tables, log and compass, estimate of wind speed, tidal streams etc.
Deviation	See the section of this book on *Navigation*.
Displacement	Archimedes (287-212 B.C.) discovered this, it gives the exact weight of a ship by measuring the exact amount of water it displaces.
Dodger	Any screen, usually made of canvas (old sail) that keeps spray out of the cabin or cuddy.
Dog house	A fixed, raised covering aft of, but attached to, cabin or cuddy.
Dragging anchor	When an anchor works loose or doesn't take a firm grip of the bottom the ship moves with tide and wind, and pulls the anchor.
Draught	The depth of a ship. She requires something more than her own draught to float in; if she is 4 ft. draught, you should hesitate to take her in less than 5 ft. charted waters; shifting sand can move more quickly than chartmakers revise their work!
Drift	The word is of OE origin and means the driving of a ship by the sea and wind with no effort to move her by those on board. Also one speaks of the drift of a current.
Ease	To slacken, to ease the sheets, means to loosen the sails, this reduces the way (momentum) of your boat. Ease her helm, when you are going to windward you put the tiller to leeward.
Ebb	The fall of the tide. OE *Ebba*.
Eddy	A circular movement in the water where a local current runs back against the mainstream. Of ON origin.
Ensign	A flag that tells us the nationality of a ship.
Eye of the Storm (Wind)	The centre of a storm; point from which the wind is blowing. Horie actually photographed the eye of a typhoon he sailed into.
Fairleads	Smooth metal tunnels that guide a rope and

	prevent it from fraying and weakening.
Fairway	A clear passage for navigation.
Fair Wind	Any wind that will permit you to take your course without tacking, also written as the book title: *Fair stood the wind for France*. 7
Fall	The loose end of a rope.
Fall away	To make too much leeway by turning her head from the wind.
False keel	Extra keel (planking) fastened externally to the real keel.
Fathom	Six feet. OE *fæfom*.
Flaw	A puff or flurry of wind as it changes direction. The word is found in modern Swedish and in Dutch, probably ON origin.
Flood	The coming of High Tide. OE *Flód*. 7
Fluke	The outermost barb of a traditional anchor. OE *Flóc*.
Foot	The bottom edge of a sail. OE *fót*.
Fore and aft	The lengthwise dimension of a ship.
For(r)ard	Sometimes *for'ard*, towards the bows of the ship.
Foresail	The sail set on the foremast.
Forestay	Wire support running from mast to stem of boat.
Foul the anchor	To catch the anchor round its own cable or any other obstacles: To foul the hawser is the same with the cable. A fouled bottom is the underbelly of a ship when coated with barnacles, marine growths etc. 4
Freeboard	The distance from deck to waterline measured on the ship's side.
Freshen	The wind is said to freshen when it gets stronger. OE *fersc*. To freshen a rope is to move it to avoid chafing.
Full and bye	To sail as close as possible to the wind while sails are still full of wind. 6
Furl sail	To roll a sail up and fasten it to its spar.
Galley	Where the ship's food is prepared.
Gang plank	The plank that permits you to get from ship to dry land. ON origin.

Gather way	To pick up speed as she moves through the water.
Ghosting	To move when there is no recognisable wind.
Gimbals	A system of suspension so that whatever the ship's position what is supported by gimbals stays perfectly and artificially horizontal.
Gingerbread	The ornamental carving on old ships was likened to the designs cooks put on their gingerbread, but for smartness the carving was usually covered with gilt, hence the expression *gilding the gingerbread*.
Go about	To tack.
Gooseneck	On the mast this is the slide fitting into which the boom is fixed.
Grapnel	Either the anchor cable or a small anchor (with 4 flukes perhaps) used to *fish up* a mooring cable, etc.
Ground tackle	Such cable, chains, etc, as are needed for putting down a mooring.
Gunwale	The upper edge of a ship's side.
Gybe	See the section on the *Three points of sailing*.
Halyard	A rope for hoisting or lowering sail.
Hand	A crew member. To hand is to furl.
Hank	Any ring or hook that fastens a jib or staysail to a stay.
Hard	A reliable piece of shore (where you shouldn't sink up to your waist in soft mud).
Hard over	(to port, to starboard) all the way over.
Hatch	The cover over the entrance to a cabin or cuddy.
Haul	To pull a rope. OE *hál*.
Hawser	Any large cable or rope.
Heads	Ship's toilet.
Headway	Forward motion of ship.
Heave	Lift, pull, haul, throw. OE *hebban*. To *heave to* means to stop.
Helm	Either the wheel or the tiller. OE *helm*.
Hoist	To haul a sail or spar aloft.
Hove to	A ship making no headway because steering and sails have been set to counteract each other.

In irons	Head into the wind, unable to move off on either tack.
In stays	Heading to the wind, but slipping from one tack to the other.
Jacob's-ladder	A rope ladder with wooden steps.
Jib	The headsail in front of the mainmast.
Jibstick	A spar for spreading out the jib.
Jury rig	Any emergency, makeshift repair arrangement, e.g. when dismasted in a storm.
Kedge	A small anchor.
Keel	The bottom of the ship from stem to stern.
Keelson	Timber placed on the keel, to which cabin floors are fixed.
Knot	One nautical mile per hour.
Laceing	Lines that fasten the sail to its spar.
Landfall	The first sight of land after a voyage. A *good* landfall means your calculations were correct, and you are where you should be.
Lay, to	To go.
Leech	See illustration on page 28.
Lee	The side towards which the wind is blowing. OE *hlé*.
Leeboard	Works on the principle of a centreboard to hinder drift to leeward.
Leeward	Down wind.
Line	Any rope used aboard ship, other than a thick cable.
Log	The book in which the daily records of position and happenings aboard ship are written.
Log	A device to tell the distance a ship has moved through the water. This gives you the speed you are making.
Luff	The edge of the sail that meets the wind first. To luff is to get so close to the wind that this edge goes floppy.
Mainsail	The chief and largest sail on the mainmast, which is the strongest and highest mast on the ship.
Making	A tide is making when it goes from the neap

	to the spring. See the section of this book dealing with *Tides*.
Marline spike	A heavy metal tool, sharp at one end, for opening ropes.
Mizzen	The second, after, mast of a ketch or yawl.
Neap	See the section of this book dealing with *Tides*.
Nip	One turn of a line round a cleat or winch.
Observed position	That plotted from bearings taken from a visible, fixed object ashore.
Offing	Open sea, used when spoken of in harbour or at safe anchorage during severe storms.
Open boat	One with no deck, cuddy or cabin.
Outboard	Beyond the sides of the ship, o/b engine or rudder is suspended from the transom.
Overfall	Roughly breaking waves where two currents etc. meet.
Painter	A rope that is used to fasten a dinghy, rowboat, etc. to shore or by which the same is towed.
Patent log	A vane on a rotating line that measures distance. See *log*.
Pay off	Permitting the boat's head to swing away from the wind.
Pay out	To let a rope loosely through the hands.
Planeing	To sail on top of the water rather than go through it; commoner with powerboats.
Plot	To plan your course over the transparent paper on top of the chart. 8
Point	Roughly 11°, actually one thirty-second part of the 360° compass. Cardinal points are North, South, East, West.
Pooped	When a following sea overtakes you and crashes down on the stern.
Portside	Lefthand side, looking forwards.
Port tack	The wind is blowing on the lefthand side, looking forwards.
Pram	Small runabout type of boat with flat ends fore and aft.
Pulpit	Guardrail at the bows of a yacht. At the stern it is called a pushpit.

Pumps	Fanciful devices for chucking water that has come aboard back in the sea; don't rely on them too much, always have a couple of buckets handy for non-stop bailing—just in case.
Quarter	Between the beam proper and the right aft position.
Race	Strong current in a locality, occurs because of the tide.
Rake	The angle of the mast to the deck, fore or aft. OE *Racian*.
Reach	See *Three points of Sailing*.
Reef	Method of reducing the area of sail exposed to the wind.
Ride	A ship is said to do this when at mooring or anchored.
Rigging	The ropes and wire stays of a ship. Those that are more or less permanent are called *standing rigging*, those intended for movement are *running rigging*.
Roach	The curve of the edge of a sail leech.
Rope	Line that is more than 1″ circumference.
Rowlocks	The metal holders for oars while rowing, usually a pivotted socket.
Rudder	Either metal or wooden plate attached by hinges to the stern; its movements direct the steering of the boat.
Sagging	Drifting carelessly to leeward. See also p. 106.
Saltings	Land that is covered by high tides, perhaps only at spring tides.
Salvage	A legal claim that *might* be put on any vessel that accepts assistance when in distress.
Scud	Thin, small low clouds fleeing before an oncoming gale. To scud along is to proceed with reduced sail in front of oncoming heavy seas and weather.
Scull	In seamen's language means to use one oar over the stern to take a boat ashore or back to ship.
Scuppers	Openings in the sides that allow water to drain off deck.

Set course	Steer for.
Shackle	Strong fastening fixed with screw or movable pin.
Sheet	A line that controls a sail OE origin.
Shrouds	Stays, usually wire, athwartships, supporting the mast.
Snub	To stop suddenly, to jerk or pull suddenly.
Soundings	To take soundings is to find out the depth of water, by leadline or echo-sounder.
Spar	A pole, mast, boom, etc. to which a sail is set. OE *gesparrian*.
Spill wind	To lose wind, become empty; said of sails.
Sprung	Any spar that has been subject to severe storms, etc, may split or become weakened, then it is sprung.
Standy by	Get ready!
Starboard	The righthand side looking forwards. Starboard tack, the wind on the right side.
Stays	The wires that keep the mast in position.
Sternway	Movement backwards, felt by a ship in irons.
Strike sails	To lower sail.
Tabernacle	The wooden housing in which the foot of the mast rests, fitted with a pivot to allow the mast to be lowered.
Tack	See illustration on page 28. For another meaning, see *Three Points of Sailing*.
Taffrail	Railing round the stern of a ship.
Tender	Small boat to get you to and from shore.
Transom	The flat stern of a boat.
Trim	The total balance, horizontally, of a ship.
Trysail	Small three-cornered sail used in stormy weather or when hove to.
Undertow	Current below the suface going a different way to a current apparent on the surface.
Veer	The change of the wind from one direction to another.
Wake	The disturbance in the water a ship creates as it passes.

Warp	A rope that tows or hauls something, e.g. a sea-anchor.
Watch	A spell of 4 hours duty while other crew members rest; very suitable for long voyages, especially in rough weather, when 4 hours' strain at a time may be all a man can take.
Weather	Colloquially, the wind.
Weigh anchor	Raise the anchor.
Whip	Twine bound round the end of a rope to stop fraying.
Winch	A small drum with rachet bar to take line or chain; also used for heavy sails.
Windlass	A larger type of winch, used to haul in an anchor.
Yacht	Originally a Dutch word for a vessel not used for commerce.
Yaw	To drift from the intended course, an error in helmsmanship.